The Religious Life of Man Series

FREDERICK J. STRENG, *Series Editor*

Texts

Understanding Religious Life, Third Edition
Frederick J. Streng

The House of Islam, Second Edition
Kenneth Cragg

Japanese Religion: Unity and Diversity, Third Edition
H. Byron Earhart

Chinese Religion: An Introduction, Third Edition
Laurence G. Thompson

The Christian Religious Tradition
Stephen Reynolds

The Buddhist Religion: A Historical Introduction, Third Edition
Richard H. Robinson and Willard L. Johnson

The Way of Torah: An Introduction to Judaism, Third Edition
Jacob Neusner

The Hindu Religious Tradition
Thomas J. Hopkins

Native American Religions: An Introduction
Sam D. Gill

African Cosmos: An Introduction to Religion in Africa
Noel Q. King

Anthologies

The Chinese Way in Religion
Laurence G. Thompson

Religion in the Japanese Experience: Sources and Interpretations
H. Byron Earhart

The Buddhist Experience: Sources and Interpretations
Stephan Beyer

The Life of Torah: Readings in the Jewish Religious Experience
Jacob Neusner

Islam from Within: Anthology of a Religion
Kenneth Cragg and R. Marston Speight

Native American Traditions: Sources and Interpretations
Sam D. Gill

African Cosmos

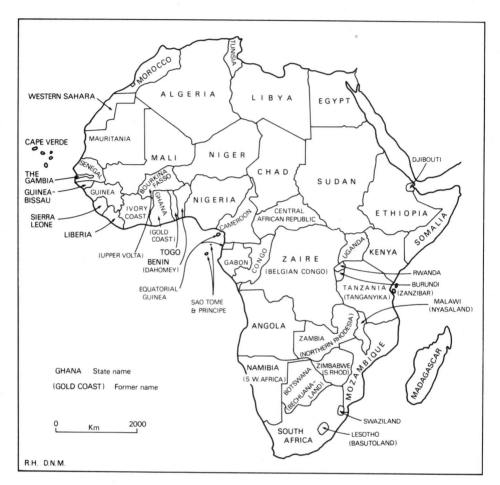

Within the map:

MOROCCO
TUNISIA
WESTERN SAHARA
ALGERIA
LIBYA
EGYPT
CAPE VERDE
MAURITANIA
THE GAMBIA
SENEGAL
GUINEA-BISSAU
GUINEA
SIERRA LEONE
LIBERIA
IVORY COAST
BOURKINA FASSO
GHANA
(GOLD COAST)
(UPPER VOLTA)
TOGO
BENIN
(DAHOMEY)
MALI
NIGER
NIGERIA
CHAD
SUDAN
DJIBOUTI
ETHIOPIA
SOMALIA
CENTRAL AFRICAN REPUBLIC
CAMEROON
EQUATORIAL GUINEA
SAO TOME & PRINCIPE
GABON
CONGO
ZAIRE
(BELGIAN CONGO)
UGANDA
KENYA
RWANDA
BURUNDI
TANZANIA
(TANGANYIKA)
(ZANZIBAR)
MALAWI
(NYASALAND)
ANGOLA
ZAMBIA
(NORTHERN RHODESIA)
ZIMBABWE
(S RHOD)
MOZAMBIQUE
MADAGASCAR
NAMIBIA
(S W AFRICA)
BOTSWANA
(BECHUANA-LAND)
SWAZILAND
SOUTH AFRICA
LESOTHO
(BASUTOLAND)

GHANA   State name
(GOLD COAST)   Former name

0   Km   2000

R.H. D.N.M.

Africa: Colonial and 1984 Political Divisions

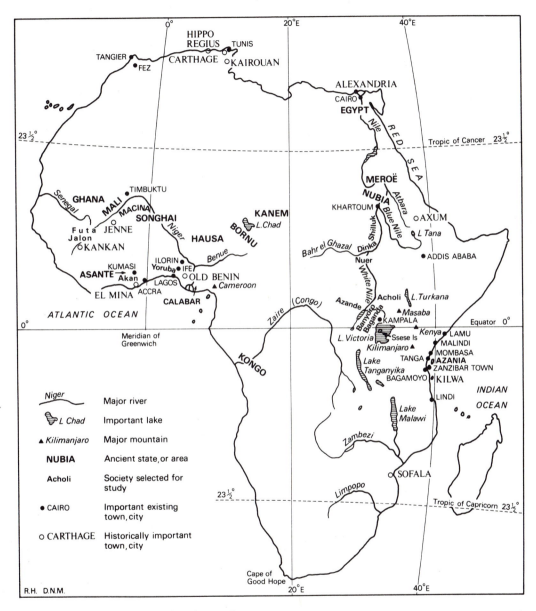

Africa: Historical and Ecological Background

African Cosmos

An Introduction
to Religion in Africa

Noel Q. King

*University of California
Santa Cruz*

Wadsworth Publishing Company
Belmont, California
A Division of Wadsworth, Inc.

Religion Editor: Sheryl Fullerton
Production Editor: Leland Moss
Managing Designer: Andrew H. Ogus
Print Buyer: Barbara Britton
Copy Editor: Gregory Gullickson
Cover: Stephen Lipke
Compositor: Weimer Typesetting Company

Printed in the United States of America
1 2 3 4 5 6 7 8 9 10—90 89 88 87 86

ISBN 0-534-05334-3

Library of Congress Cataloging in Publication Data

King, Noel Quinton.
 African cosmos.

 Bibliography: p.
 Includes index.
 1. Africa—Religion. I. Title.
BL2400.K49 1986   291′.096   85-5378
ISBN 0-534-05334-3

Contents

Dedication and Thanks

On my sixty-first birthday I dedicate this book to my teachers, colleagues, and students in India/Pakistan, Britain, the United States, and Papua/New Guinea. First, I have to thank the four African colleagues who read the manuscript and brought about two rewritings—Reverend Professor J. Omosade Awolalu of the University of Ibadan, Nigeria; Professor J. S. Pobee of Legon University, Ghana; Dr. Abdu B. Kasozi of the University of Khartoum, Sudan; and Reverend Professor A. Byaruhanga T. Akiiki-Mujaju of Makerere University. I discussed the Dinka-Acholi material with Dr. p'Bitek Okot, and my debt to his thought is apparent. The illness he died of should not necessarily have been fatal, but because of security difficulties he could not be taken to medical help. May he rest in peace. I thank my other teachers and collaborators in Africa, moving from west to east: Harry Sawyerr, William Conton, Kwesi Dickson, Mercy Yamoah, Christian Gaba, William Abraham, Kwabena Nketia, Yusufu Lule, Eunice Posnansky, Aloysius Lugira, Semakula Kiwanuka, Ahmed Khaab Nsambo, Seyyid Akhtar Rizvi, Lenny D'Almeida, Yasmin and Azim Nanji, Robin Lamburn, Said Hamdun, Martin Mbwana, Jerome Bamunoba, and Dunstan Nsubuga.

In the United Kingdom a number of Africanists have been of assistance with this work, including Harold Turner, Andrew Walls, Adrian Hastings, Hannah Stanton, Louise Pirouet, Jan Knappert, and Fred Welbourn. The map was drawn up from my incoherent notes by Dr. William McMaster, a former Makerere colleague now at Edinburgh. The photographs of Akan mediums and Nuer sacrifice are from the collection in the Pitt Rivers Museum at Oxford, which Mrs. Elizabeth Edwards of the library there researched for me with immense patience despite my dithering. Mrs. Ruth Leech, wife of the inspired teacher who taught me metropolitan English when I first came from India, kindly read the manuscript and made many beneficial suggestions. I remain ever indebted to those who have patiently helped me to enjoy something of the immense ocean of German Africanistics: Dr. Ernst Dammann at Hamburg; Professors Horst Buerkle of Munich and H. W. Gensichen of Heidelberg; and Herr Gerhard Lasko of Berlin.

I recall with reverence and thanks those of my Africa gurus who have journeyed to the land of the spirit ancestors: Hamisi Katumbhoi, J.W.T. Allen, Kofi Busia, Kofi Antuban, Alex Kyerematten, S. H. Bonsu Abban, S. G. Williamson, Janani Luwum, Comfort Opare, and others unnamed.

I thank those in the United States who have read, critiqued, and improved this work—Professor Christine Downing, Laurie R. King, Dr. Charles Long, David Esterline, Willard Johnson, Evan M. Zeusse, David Crummey, a good number of my undergraduate students, as well as the indefatigable editor of the series, Dr. Fred Streng, without whose continual resuscitation this baby would have died the natural death it may have deserved.

A word of thanks for the artwork. The pen and ink sketches of Èṣù and of the old woman before the ancestors are by Professor Kenneth C. Orrett of West Valley College. The photographs of the Akuaba dolls, Sasabonsam, Ddungu, and the umbilical cords are by Laurie King. The Gisu initiations were photographed by Professor Horst Buerkle of Munich and are published with his permission. The bibliography, the maps, and the reading that lie behind this work owe much to the interlibrary loan department, the reference desk, and the maps and recordings sections of the McHenry Library on our Santa Cruz campus of the University of California. Here are but a few of the people concerned: Rex Beckham, Catherine Borka, Pedro Cosmé, Al Eickhoff, Margaret Felts, Joan Hodgson, Jacqueline Marie, Ken McKenzie, Janet Pumphrey, Elizabeth (Betty) Rentz, Alan Ritch, Margaret Robinson, Judith Steen, Stan Stevens, and Marion Taylor; all have been of help beyond the call of duty. My wonder-working research assistant, John Grinnell, has done marvels. I thank "B" Stickney for help with the index.

At various times over the years our campus research grants committee of the academic senate has made grants for research that was done for its own pure uselessness and that no other giver would touch. I confess that I have used numerous by-products in this book. Thanks are due to such true patrons of scholarship.

The material concerning women in Africa that is distributed throughout the book goes back mainly to the notebooks of Evelyn King, who worked in Africa from 1956 to 1968. She died in 1972 on her way back from fieldwork in the Punjab. The material has been updated in the light of newer research and in consultation with our colleagues and former students, including Winifred Allen, Irene Anderson, Esther Awolalu,

Christine Downing, Magdalen Gathi, Hannah Kinoti, Laurie King, Her Highness the Nnabugereka, Mercy Amba Odudoye, Louise Pirouet, and Hannah Stanton. I also thank hosts and colleagues in French- and Portuguese-speaking Africa who have provided guidance, hospitality, and direction in reading. I have shamelessly used insights gained thereby without acknowledgment beyond this heartfelt thanks.

I thank Peggy Vecchione, Kay Martinez, and Bernadette O'Meara for their typing and other help. I am indebted to Sheryl Fullerton for patiently gearing the hard facts of commercial publishing to my world of academic dreaming, and to her colleagues, including Leland Moss, the production editor, as well as the typesetters and printers. The copy editor, Gregory Gullickson, has gone far beyond the call of duty in reducing my thoughts, vocabulary, and style to the American norm. These abbreviated lists omit many, especially traditionalists and students, whose names do not immediately come to my rather defective memory but whose grace remains with me. The lists also show why I see myself as a compiler rather than an author.

This book should have been written by an African who had lived sufficient of his or her adult years in Africa and then taught for a comparable period in America. Such people are too rare, busy, and important to do this work. Instead it has been written by a person of Pakistani origin who has spent thirteen years teaching and researching in Africa, and a comparable length of time in the U.S.A. Perhaps not many South Asians have turned to this kind of work, but a person with a background in Hinduism, Islam, and non-Western Christianity may have something to contribute.

I have focused the detailed studies presented in this book on three large, strategically located, anglophone (English-using) areas in equatorial Africa that yield a paradigm or pattern for study. Students should turn from this introductory text directly to books written by Africans from those societies that use English as a first or second language. Guidance for American readers of French will be found in the bibliography.

As in any field, words can take on either distinction or stench as usage changes. Thus *Hamitic*, which was once a convenient label for certain peoples (*tribes* is a "no-no") is definitely out, and *Nilotic* is on its way out. Where I deal with some of the peoples who belong to the latter group, I have used *Luo river-lake people*, which may arouse the ire of some anthropologists and linguists, but will not submit Africans to any possibly racist theories. *Bantu* is a glorious African word meaning "the human beings, the people," rather like the Navaho *Dine*, and I could not bear to abandon it to the rulers of South Africa who use it to indicate something derogatory. I apologize for any offensive words left in through ignorance or weakness or inserted by overly zealous helpers.

I do not know whether I ought to apologize to modern scholars for mentioning some of their confrontations and arguments but not giving many names or details. While students must be made aware of the heated discussions that are going on, they need not be bombarded with names that at this stage are irrelevant. I have indicated a little of this state of controversy in mentioning the debate over *ntuism* (p. 32) and the arguments over the nature of God in African thought (p. 33 and many other places). Students need not get more deeply involved at first, but soon will if they wish to work with the literature I cite in the bibliography.

In thanking these friends and making these apologies, I do not wish to attribute the faults and defects in this book to any but myself, though I would claim the indulgence and privileges granted to a *Mzee*, an elder. It is difficult for a scholar to keep in touch with the latest developments in any field, and this is even more true when dealing with the African continent, which sees some of the most rapid and dramatic changes of any area on earth. For example, the horror and agony of the famine that is overtaking the continent has only come to light since the basic text of this book was completed in early 1983. I fear I have not been able to take into account one of the worst calamities in human history. This fact overshadows anything I can say.

Royalties from this book will help subsidize publications originating in Africa. I lay this *mala* or garland of Punjabi pomegranate flowers and jasmine blossoms grown in California at the feet of the Black Mother who tries to bring to birth a truer humanity, in the hope that her love, being, and power may be made known to others.

NOEL Q. KING
Freedom, California
Christmas Day, 1983

African Cosmos

Introduction

WHY STUDY AFRICAN RELIGION?

Like some great question mark at the center and crossroads of the world stands Africa. Our best available scientific information tells us that the human race originated there. Probably we humans lingered in Africa for thousands of years before moving off to the ends of the earth, and during that time we developed much that is now common to human thought and life wherever they are found.

Africa is then in some sense the mother of us all—indeed, of all civilization. She has in every epoch contributed to world civilization. Our Western parochialism causes us to forget that ancient Egypt, for thousands of years in the forefront of human endeavor, was African. A thousand years after the Greeks and Romans had annexed Egypt and themselves gone into decline, African civilizations deeply affected Islamic world culture and produced thinkers and explorers of world renown. In the thirteenth century, Ibn Khaldun produced a world history that has not been surpassed. Ibn Battuta of Tangier, in the North African far west, was acclaimed the greatest traveler of the age. He visited Arabia, central Asia, India, Indonesia, and China, and described flourishing black civilizations in both eastern and western tropical Africa. He was by language and culture "Arab," and was proud to say that he was of the Luwata tribe, a subgroup of the Berbers (who go back in Africa to the beginning of history).

In the centuries that followed, black Africa suffered the slave trades from western Asia and eastern Europe, from Arabia and India, from western Europe and the Americas. She yielded some of her best to build up others. Suffering, according to all the great religions, is the stuff of human growth, and Africa has accumulated capital in the world bank of suffering that none, not even the Jews, can surpass. She has undergone invasion and subjugation by colonialism, then by economic neo-colonialism, which has reduced some of the richest peoples in the world to destitution.

In 1960, the *annus mirabilis* of African freedom, the death-knell of the colonial insult was ringing, and new African countries were being every-where proclaimed. Those of us who were so fortunate as to be there— "to be young . . . and in that dawn to be alive . . ."—were confident that the whole world would pay attention and turn respectfully to learn from this person who, even when stripped naked, sold down the river by black and white brothers, and maltreated, still retained immense dignity, inscrutable wisdom, and—mysteriously enough—love and for-giveness. Twenty-five years later it is hard not to be bitter and to think, "Had an African country kidnapped a hundred American anthropolo-gists and imprisoned them unharmed for a year . . ." or "Had Africa held the world to ransom by threatening to cut off supply of the rare and precious minerals on which the world economy depends . . . ."

This little book represents an attempt to listen to Mother Africa's deepest wisdom. For the greatest part of human history, the best minds have put their finest thinking into religious studies, and Africans are no exception. If we want to know the world in which we live, and above all the world in which our children will live, it is essential to study the distillation, the quintessence, of African woman and man's ultimate questioning—their religion.

A WORD ON METHOD

There are hundreds of cultural units and languages in Africa; the religion of each has in it something priceless and unique. The religion of one small group may be as different from that of its close neighbor as Chris-tianity is from Judaism. It is impossible in a small book to generalize about hundreds of religions. To treat them as all the same, then assem-ble their phenomena under agreed headings, may be a wonderful method of studying bugs and butterflies, but not things human. Yet, having spent over thirty years studying African religions (thirteen of those years in Africa), I am continually impressed by how much spiritual unity there is amid African diversity. Accordingly, this book presents six major religious systems that geographically bestride equatorial Africa, black Africa proper, from west to east; through kindred religious sys-tems they reach out to the rest of Africa and the world. In each case I have chosen religions that I have studied at the feet of African scholars who are deeply versed in those religions and who know Western ways of thought and scholarship. In each case I try to let the African religion be set forth in the way its own traditionalists and scholars explain it. The resultant framework is as follows:

Two West African religious systems:

1. The Yoruba of Nigeria

2. For comparison and juxtaposition, the Akan of Ghana

The religious world of Bantu-speaking peoples:

1. The religion of the Ganda

2. The religion of the Swahili

Religions of the "Luo" river-lake peoples:

1. The Dinka and Nuer

2. The Acholi

At this point the reader has before him or her representative examples of African traditional religion taken from right across equatorial Africa, the heartland of the black world. Each system connects with cultures and civilizations that sweep across the continent and the world. The Yoruba and Akan systems reach to the west and north, through the Kwa languages, and link with groups that reach up toward the Niger bend and the Atlantic coast. Through the involuntary migrations of millions, they have reached and are still active in Cuba, Brazil, and the United States. These religions are also outstanding in that over a period of years they have produced African theologians who know their own traditions from inside and have written books that are accessible to world audiences. The first university professorial chairs in the world devoted to the study of African religion were established thirty years ago in Nigeria and Ghana.

The East African systems described link with the religions of the Bantu-speaking peoples, who have settled from Nigeria to the Cape of Good Hope and right across Africa from the Indian Ocean to the southern Atlantic. The Arab slave trade carried Bantu influence to India and the whole of western Asia. The Bantu also came in large numbers to the Americas. Here and in Asia, they became famous as rebels, workers, soldiers, and the mothers of sultans and imams. Here again, the works of African scholars are accessible to the reader. The universities of East Africa were not far behind West Africa in their attention to these studies.

Connecting these two great arcs of religious thought that stretch across Africa are the religions of the Luo-speaking river-lake peoples, from ocean to ocean and from the equator to Land's End.[1] Here again,

---

[1] For Europeans on the way to the Orient "Land's End" was a Cape of Good Hope; to Africans it is the end of their continent.

indigenous writers can be our guide, and some of the best European thinkers of this century have written classic works on these religions. Archaeology has also shown that the culture of which these peoples may be a remnant is very old and widespread, stretching far north and westward into what is now the Sahara, with other influential remnants far away in West Africa.

Having studied these major systems in all of their diversity, a student is able to recognize their unity and can only then legitimately look for a paradigm, a pattern. (As the Zen master teaches: "Before enlightenment—mountains, trees, and streams. After enlightenment—mountains, trees, and streams.") Indeed, a basic pattern, system, and framework for concepts does emerge. The main elements in the lively and ever-changing pattern of interaction are fairly easy to identify, though their proportions, interactions, and juxtaposition at different moments defy description. The point of departure is anthropocentric; the central and ultimate concern is with woman and man, their fullness of being and power, their health in the widest sense. Around this center ellipses of light come into and out of focus. Coordinate with them are circles of darkness, yet they are all one in love, life, and power. The elements we must fit into this interweaving include:

Doctrines about God

The greater and lesser spirits

The ancestors

The human being

"The faceless powers"—sorcery, magic, "fetishes," certain prayers, blessings, and curses

Means of fellowship with the spirit—prayer, mysticism, divination, sacrifice, rituals (especially of life's turning points)

Following a chapter devoted to these last topics, Christianity and Islam are studied, focusing on their long history in Africa and their interaction with traditional religion (and with each other).

The earliest heartlands of Christianity after Palestine and Syria were in the countryside of Egypt and Roman Africa. Some of Christianity's basic (and greatest) thinkers came from Africa. The prophet Muhammad's first muezzin (caller to prayer) was a black. Islam had crossed Africa to the Atlantic within a generation of the Prophet's death, and by the sixteenth century had deeply penetrated most of Africa north and south of the Sahara, though it had not yet effectively entered the equatorial regions. In the nineteenth century Islam revived, faced the difficulties of incoming non-Muslim governments, and then found means of resuming its expansion under foreign colonial rule.

In the nineteenth century Christianity tried for the third time in Africa.[2] Its second attempt had been ruined by the slave trade and internal problems in Europe. Its third attempt was soon overtaken by European colonial intrusion. Although Christianity found ways of using these outside forces, association with such forces has not been easy to shake off in modern times, when Christianity has become indigenous and the forces have been thrown out. But Christianity is succeeding, and the pulsating life not only of "mainline" Roman Catholic and Protestant African-led churches but of the "churches of African initiative" tells its own story for the future of world Christianity, as the Church's center of gravity shifts from Europe and North America to Africa, Latin America, and the Pacific.

The religious significance of Marxism in Africa is tentatively assessed, especially in light of the African desire to be positively nonaligned and the African Christian refusal to accept that Marxism, let alone socialism, is necessarily better or worse than other forms of materialism.

We end by saying something of the three religions in their modern circumstance of transcendent achievement and hope, despite neo-colonialism and renewed suffering, especially in South Africa. Maps and an annotated bibliography give the student the means to make full use of this book as an introduction and to proceed to further study, possible field work, and all manner of experiential learning of a continent that will undoubtedly play a great role in our future.

---

[2] She had tried in the first seven centuries, and again from the fifteenth to seventeenth.

CHAPTER 1

The Religious World of the Yoruba

An ancient traditional people of tropical Africa, the Yoruba have always been one of the biggest religious groups in Africa; today they number perhaps fifteen million. Although they have no representative as such at the United Nations, the Yoruba are of profound importance in matters of world civilization: They are an integral part of Africa's most powerful country, Nigeria, and have considerable numbers in neighboring lands like Benin (Dahomey). People of their culture coming originally as involuntary immigrants have remained to influence Brazil (where they are known as "Nago"), Cuba ("Lucumi"), and Sierra Leone ("Aku"), not to mention Jamaica, the United States, North Africa, and the Islamic world, whither many were also carried in slavery. Certainly no other African group has contributed so much to the culture of the Americas.

West to east, the Yoruba inhabit the rain forest and lagoon country of West Africa from Benin (Dahomey) to the beginning of the creeks of the Niger Delta; south to north, from the sea up into the savannah grasslands. Because Yoruba country possesses little high land and is not far from the equator, it is hot all the year round; however, because it is not too far from the sea it never attains the murderous heat of some inland places. They get a heavy rainfall in June, July, and September, whilst December through February tends to be dry. Yams, corn, beans, bananas, cassava, and taro grow abundantly, and coffee, cocoa, and palm products provide cash crops for export. Chickens, goats, pigs, ducks, and turkeys forage and multiply everywhere; the rivers, lagoons, and sea provide fish.

The tonal language of the Yoruba emphasizes the shade and sound of meaning, which explains their love of puns, fun for them but a series of ludicrous snares and pitfalls for the foreigner. For an English, French, German, or Spanish speaker, to understand Yoruba is about as easy as to understand Chinese, since the problem of script does not arise. Yoruba is one of the Kwa languages (including Igbo, Ewe, Gã, Akan, and Kru), part of a great group of languages that sweep across Africa from Nigeria to the Atlantic. The common features of these languages indicate some cultural, historical, and religious affinity. The Kwa languages in turn are part of the Niger-Congo branch of the Congo-Kordofanian family. (The river names are obvious; Kordofan is an area in the Sudan.)

For centuries the Yoruba have loved living together in towns. Although they trace their clan and family structure through their male ancestors, they also deem important an individual's female ancestors, so far as they can be remembered. After marriage a woman usually moves to her husband's or his father's house. Her children of both sexes are included in the man's clan. Her son's children are members of that clan, too, while her daughter's children join that of their father. In the old days it increased a man's power if he was able to take and maintain a number of wives, especially since women, besides handling the domestic work and producing children, did much of the farming, marketing, and business.

The Yoruba civilization met the onslaught of the slave trades across both the Sahara and the Atlantic. It survived despite centuries of slaving and civil wars that carried off the cream of the young men and women. Physically, in matters of reproduction after decimation and in overcoming sheer agony and suffering, the Yoruba must be amongst the most gifted in the world. In their festivals and dance and in the making of brilliant art, they are also among the most prolific. In their mythology, metaphysics, and theology, that is, their thinking about life's ultimates, as we shall see, they are second to none.

Understanding the Yoruba culture is important because the Yoruba have produced a religious system that is of universal human significance and survives into the modern world. Islam and Christianity, modern urbanization and technology, industrial revolutions old and new, as well as modern Western thought have all been met and rejected or absorbed. Readers who have been mainly trained in English and Western forms of education can here get acquainted with a civilization whose spokespersons are themselves Yoruba, yet who are highly accomplished in Western ways. Here is an introduction to an African culture that a reader can check out and supplement by consulting the masterworks as they were written by Yoruba using English in the first place. This chapter presents a compendium of teaching by internationally recognized Yoruba teachers, given in the personal form (*we, our*) as they spoke it.

THE YORUBA SUPREME BEING
AND THE MYTH OF CREATION

We begin with the Supreme Being, the Almighty, who was so readily recognized as Allah or God when Islam and Christianity came this way. Some wise ones have wondered whether the innermost name of our God can be spoken, as in the case of the Hebrew *Jehovah*. God is given various names, and, like the people of the Old Testament and the Qur'an, elders love to combine them in different syllables to produce meanings that describe our manifold thoughts on God. It is a delight and a nourishment to the soul to ponder the ancient names of God we find in sayings and myths, to meditate lovingly on the many names and attributes of God enshrined in the proverbs that have been handed down from our primordial past. Frequently we hear *Olórun Olódùmarè*. To a Yoruba this signifies the Supreme and Eternal Being who dwells in the Heavens, One who is all powerful and all trustworthy. He is *Alààyè*, the One who Lives, *Elémìì* the Lord of Life. Yoruba usually say, "I shall do this or that . . . if the Lord of Life does not recall it (my life)," an indication that we solely depend upon the Supreme Being for life's activities and achievements.

Another title for God, *Ẹlẹ́dàá* or Creator, links up naturally with our creation myth. In the town of Ilé-Ifè, where some of our traditions tell us that divine powers first descended, elders will recite the myths for us in the proper way. The spiritual emanations and atmosphere of that place enable our souls to perceive and understand better, for no myth can be fully understood outside of its context in ritual and sacred space.

> When Olódùmarè and certain divinities resided in the heavens above, the earth was like a marsh and wasteland. Heaven and earth were not far apart, and the inhabitants of the above came at times to earth to take their pastimes and hunting herein. When Olódùmarè made the decision to cause firm land to appear, he called Òrìsà-ńlá (Great-divinity) and commanded him to carry out this design. He provided him with some soil, a hen with five toes, and a pigeon. Òrìsà-ńlá came to earth, threw down the soil, and released the birds. The hen spread the soil, the waters were driven back, dry land appeared. When the land was wide and firm enough, Olódùmarè sent Òrìsà-ńlá to place trees upon the earth. The first trees were the palm and three others that provide food, drink, shade, and shelter.
>
> Olódùmarè then breathed life into sixteen human beings and sent them to earth. He taught Òrìsà-ńlá how to make the forms of human beings, after which Olódùmarè himself would give them life.

This is only one form of the myth. At Ilé-Ifè there exists a parallel version, in which Òrìsà-ńlá gets drunk on palm wine and the materials God has given him are stolen by another divinity, Odùduwà, who becomes the creator. To apply the conclusions reached by modern critical study of myths in the Bible and in other literature, one could say that the various versions are connected with different "tribal" groups, different sanctuaries and holy places. Some versions may be classified as "aetiological," that is, they answer the question "Why?": "Why is palm wine a 'no-no' in the cult of this deity?" "Why is Odùduwà treated as a creator by some while others think of Òrìṣà-ńlá as creator?" "This is a race in which everyone gets prizes"—actually both assisted in the work of creation.

Modern Western students who are educated to memorize scientific textbooks and treat each word as literal, exclusive truth often find it hard to understand myth. They ask questions like, "If the earth was not formed and animals not yet created, where and what did the divine beings hunt?" Myth has its own methods of interpretation, just as scientific textbooks have theirs and poetry its own. A Yoruba theologian likes to bring out a few inferences that may be legitimately drawn from the myth. The first is the absoluteness of Olódùmarè. He is the One and Only, the All Powerful, the Giver of Life. Each one of these inferences is abundantly substantiated by Yoruba popular titles for God and by many expressions in proverbs. He is transcendent, high and lifted up, but yet he cares for every detail. We see in this myth "signifiers" of two other metaphors that describe Ọlọ́run-Olódùmarè. He is like a king—commander, director, and judge; the divinities and all creation comprise his court. He is like a father: We come from him, but he is senior to us all. He cares for everything, yet is remote, calm, balanced in judgment. Metaphors should not be pressed too far or overemphasized: Societies that (unlike the Yoruba) detest kingship and make fatherhood a joke may be more hindered than helped.

THE DIVINITIES, THE ÒRÌṢÀ

In the creation myth, the Òrìṣà appeared. The intense interest of some Yoruba in the Òrìṣà and their activities may lead them to speak as if the Òrìṣà were deities in themselves. Because of this, the Yoruba have been accused by Muslims and Christians of being polytheists, and by anthropologists and old-fashioned comparative religionists of believing in a High God who is otiose. *Otiose* could be loosely defined as "superfluous, out of circuit, supernumerary," indicating a God who is honored every now and then in speech and piety but has no services, no temple, no being in real life. In our traditional religion if he has no services or ministers of his own, that is because the divinities are only his attributes, his messengers, his agents. He is in our every thought and deed, and frequently on our lips; always his being and omnipresence are implied, and the divinities do not subsist except in him.

The Òrìṣà, then, are the emanations of God's powers, his functioning in certain aspects of his activity as understood by humans. Some are the "personifications" of God's powers in nature, the earth, the rivers, the lagoons, the seas. Some are beings who lived as humans long ago, their divinity recognized later by their descendants. Having 201 or 1,700 Òrìṣà does not make the Yoruba rank polytheists, but simply underlines the wealth of their religious thought.

The Archdivinity

We met the Òrìṣà par excellence, the archdivinity, among the primordial beings used in creation. In Ibadan and Ilé-Ifẹ̀ he is called Òrìṣà-ńlá, but frequently he is also called Ọbàtálá. He is the shaper, the former, who makes and molds the babe in the womb. The so-called deformed or misshapen are his also, for he created them so for a purpose. To mock them is to mock him. His color is white. His sacrament is the bringing of pure water to his sanctuary by a pure virgin or pure old woman. She rings a bell before her as she goes to the spring and as she returns. She may greet no one by the way. At the shrine this water is given as a blessing to worshippers. The offerings made there are without bloodshed. In one tradition Ọbàtálá and Odùduwá are treated as androgynous, that is, both male and female. It is perhaps extreme to see in these traditions the takeover of female traditions by a male cult, as was the case in Zeus's overshadowing of the Athene traditions in Greece. But at least they indicate that the Yoruba tendency to overuse the masculine pronouns for the divine is custom rather than sexism, for the divine is neither male nor female, but both—and beyond both.

The Divinity of Divination and Prognostics

Ọrúnmìlá was sent with the creator to give guidance. According to tradition, he continues this work in both heaven and earth. His oracle can be "read" to discover where the enquirer stands with regard to the forces of the divine and human world. It is not possible in this brief survey to describe fully the Ifá oracle-method, but only to say that this Òrìṣà's shrine is found in most traditional households. The sixteen palm nuts in their lidded bowl, the tray and tappers for divining, and other emblems and paraphernalia of this divinity are kept in a curtained corner. Daily or on the first day of every week (the Yoruba traditional week was one of four days) the shrine is revealed and the appropriate rites performed by the priest. His title is Babaláwo, "the father of mysteries." This has crossed the ocean to Haiti as Papaloi.

Èṣù, the Prankster

Closely associated with the Supreme Being and with Ọrúnmìlà and his oracle is Èṣù (see Figure 1.1). Too easily he was aligned by some Muslims and Christians with Satan, and seen by anthropologists as "the Trickster." There is no dualism in Yoruba tradition, where all is of God. Yet God has depths and subtleties we cannot plumb. The divine, human, and natural universe has forces we cannot understand. Because

Figure 1.1   Èṣù, the Yoruba "prankster." (Drawing by Kenneth C. Orrett)

we do not understand, we hate, fear, and revolt from much in the play of the spirit and the other forces around us. Èṣù is the one who knows, who can make known, who can test, try, probe. He is our messenger to the world above, bringing word thence to us. He is everywhere observing and reporting to the divine, organizing morality and piety by any means. He will create jealousy between co-wives and friends to refine their characters. He will deceive people into wrong behavior so they may gain favor by their expiation and feed the divinities with their offerings.

The representations and icons of Èṣù appear everywhere in the traditional Yoruba world. These may be a human-shaped mud figure with horns on its head and a club or knife nearby, or a mere hunk of crumbling stone pushed into the earth, or an inverted pot with a hole in it. In decorative art he may be represented by a phallus, while in fable and common talk he is a little person who is pompously aware of his shortness. One may flatter him (for a moment) by calling him "he who is so tall he towers over the pea-nut trees." Èṣù's avoidance is palm kernel oil, but he likes palm oil. If you want him to chase your enemy, give him the former while naming your enemy, and then after a pause give him some of the latter while naming yourself. His offerings include dogs, he-goats, chickens, and palm wine.

Ṣàngó, King and Thunderer

Ṣàngó was an early Aláààfin (king) of Ọ̀yọ́, and the Yoruba tell many legends about him. His wives and his subjects were forever quarreling among themselves and troubling the king. He rode off into the forest, went up into the sky, and rules by using thunder and lightning. According to other legends, he was a tyrant much given to the study of magic. He was forced to abdicate, and as he went into exile he hanged himself in a tree. During certain festivals or sometimes when there is thunder, to propitiate Ṣàngó people will cry out, "The king did not hang." When a person is killed by lightning, this is believed to be divine retribution, and he or she is not given the burial of a decent person. A house that has been struck cannot be used until a sacrifice has been offered there and various payments made.

There are shrines to Ṣàngó in most parts of Yorubaland. He is sometimes represented in human form along with three smaller people, who may be his wives. Objects that indicate his presence, representations of which appear also as his art forms, are rams, the double-headed axe, gourd rattles, inverted food mortars, and celts or "thunder-stones" in a water pot. His color is purple or maroon. His offering is *orógbó*, bitter kola (*garcinia gnetiodes*). He also likes palm oil and chickens.

People "mounted by Ṣàngó," that is, into whom Ṣàngó has entered, will dance to the little *bata* drum and tell forth the will of the divine. Very often they are men with women's hairdos, wearing red cotton coats covered with cowries and charms. This kind of spirit-possession is not confined to this divinity, nor indeed to the Yoruba world; it is a complex topic that deserves separate treatment. The same may be said of festival days and holy days, which abound for all the Yoruba divinities. Luckily, for those who cannot experience such a celebration, the Yoruba also produce much religious art, and their carvings may be seen in many parts of the world.

When the German scholar Frobenius came to study in Yorubaland at the beginning of this century, he was amazed at the high standards of Yoruba thought and aesthetics, considering the European stereotypes about "barbaric peoples." He faithfully recorded many parallels between classical Greek and Roman civilization and the Yoruba. Though he later explained them away, it is fascinating to consider his idea that this part of Africa is somehow connected with the Atlantis myth. (Without some hypothesis of common origins, it is difficult to discuss or explain the relationship of Ṣàngó, who has a double axe and hangs himself, to Thor and Woden. The two Norse gods are closely connected to one another. Thor wields a hammer and Woden hangs himself.) Besides excelling as sculptors, metaphysicians, and philosophers, the classical Yoruba were much devoted to disciplined city and state government and were forced by circumstances to be skilled in the science of war.

Ogún, Divinity of War and Iron

Ogún is the Yoruba's Mars, a divinity of war. According to the myths he has never been welcome or at home among the Yoruba. He is on the edge of society, and his power to kill and destroy can be turned at any moment against his own people. He is beyond control, but luckily he grows disgusted with his deeds and goes away. But Ogún is not just a god of war: He is patron of the hunter and forester. In the background of our thought the wild man of the wasteland remains frightening and fascinating, an uncivilized killer. Yet he is an innovator; he knows what is going on in other societies, as well as what the spirits of the skies and the woods and grasslands teach. Women can attract him, domesticate him, and put him to service.

Ogún is also connected with iron. Where two pieces of iron are put together and his name called upon them, Ogún is there. Many centuries ago the Iron Age revolution took place in Black Africa. Today the blacksmith is given special treatment in many places. He lives on the edge of society, and while he works he must refrain from sexual contact, for he is carrying out a religious rite. Inheriting the centuries-old skills of his family, the master blacksmith possesses great knowledge not only of technology but of basic human thought. Perhaps that is why the complex metallurgical processes and alloys discovered by African smiths of past centuries were used in sacred ceremonies and regalia rather than in firearms and engines. Iron helped not only our warriors but also our farmers and our mighty migrations across the continent. Even so, in our traditional times we did not rape the earth and the forest, nor look on the trees, forests, rivers, and mountains as enemies against whom to wage war.

Reverence for Ogún is one of the traditional cults which has survived and gathered new strength. Ogún is recognized as the patron of all those who use iron. Thus barbers, circumcisers, surgeons, taxi and truck drivers, and machine operators are coming to revere the power of iron, which can help us do what we want but can also suddenly inflict the most dreadful and apparently irrational punishment—blood and carnage seemingly for its own sake. From the human point of view and at our level of existence, some aspects of the divine are wrathful, merciless, unpredictable. The Yoruba do not hesitate to say so in their myths and ceremonies, for there is no point in pretending to believe otherwise. But they insist that there is more to be said.

The Farmer Divinity

Until recently the Yoruba were a nation of farmers. The patron of the Yoruba farmer is Òrìṣà-oko, another divinity whose characteristics are both female and male. A wife and her husband left their hometown

Figure 1.2   In many parts of the ancient world twins were killed at birth. The Yoruba have one of the highest human twinning birthrates. Long ago they too practised twin infanticide. Then an oracle told them to cherish twins and to make effigies of them, by which they reverenced the spirit-principle of the twins. These statues are called ere ibeji. *(Should we make and reverence wooden effigies of bombs?) (Photo: Laurie R. King)*

because the husband had developed a terrible disease. In their exile she gathered fruit and discovered how to plant the fruit trees and grow more fruit. He hunted animals and birds and learned the properties of edible herbs and leaves. Thus he became cured of his disease, and they were able to go home. They taught their fellow citizens their skills, and in due time they and their body of knowledge were treated as divinity. We still do not know which of the couple is Òrìṣà-oko, whose ministry is open to women as well as men. The honey bee is its special creature. As you can easily imagine, the communion feasts of this divinity are especially noteworthy for the variety of luscious foods and drinks offered.

The Earth, Our Mother

Although it would be instructive to study each Yoruba divinity (for example, see Figure 1.2), we must pass over ever so many others to focus on one who stands apart from and underlies them all: Ilẹ, the earth. She is one of the primordial beings, for in the creation myth we are not told that the Òrìṣà coming from heaven created the earth, but that they used a five-toed chicken to spread the bag of soil they had brought so that they could establish the dry land, which is she. At birth we rest on her, at death we are placed in her womb, and at every meal the ancestors who dwell in her are honored with a few drops of drink poured on the ground.

Once long ago Ilẹ́ and a heavenly being were hunting. They hunted all day, but all they took was one rodent, and they quarreled over the prey. When Ilẹ́'s companion took it with him to heaven, Ilẹ́ denied her blessing of increase to everything. Green things failed, living things ceased to multiply. All things divine and natural begged the heavenly being to give in. He did so, and Earth relented.

It is unfortunately not true that modern Yoruba respect the earth more than their Western counterparts. They too are willing to refuse to face pollution so long as they go on benefiting from modernization and development. But this story of Earth and her power reminds them and us what defiance of Earth and what ecological disaster mean.

The Ògbóni Society and Its Art

Closely connected with the Earth is the Ògbóni cult, called "secret society" by those who love to whisper about the esoteric. It indeed has its secrets, but in the old days before governments tried to suppress it, it was public enough. Older men and women who had attained eminence and a reputation for integrity joined it. It restrained the king and the supreme council, as well as the hierarchies of priests and warlords, from committing arbitrary acts, and it brought fights and skirmishes to arbitration.

Ògbóni art is different from most Yoruba art; it has been called iconic (in the sense of the icons of the Russian Church), hieratic (having to do with the priestly), and monumental (as opposed to vibrating with movement). Its members have followed the Òrìṣà and their ways all through life. Now their thoughts have gone on to the founts of stillness and repose that come from Mother Earth.

OTHER ASPECTS OF THE YORUBA RELIGION

Because so much in Yoruba art, folklore, mythology, and ceremony is connected with the Òrìṣà and related cults, it is easy for the Òrìṣà to take on undue prominence in the student's mind. The worship of God remains preeminent, but there is also the reverence toward the ancestors and the attention to other powers.

The Foremothers and Forefathers

Some African scholars prefer to speak of the ancestors as "the living dead," that is, fathers and mothers who have passed on from the daily, active life of ordinary human beings but have not yet merged with those dead and forgotten. (I believe "lively dead" conveys the idea better.) For the Yoruba, the human being consists of *ara* (matter) molded by Òrìṣà-ńlá. Into this Olódùmarè breathes *èmi*, spirit. The Yoruba word for the soul may be *òkan* (strictly speaking, "the heart"), or as some have rendered it, *orì-inú*, the "inner head," the inner controlling being of a person. When someone dies and the body returns to earth, the constituents given by God return whither they came, and their elements are "reincarnated" in the children to be born.

Festival Dances for the Lively Dead

When people die, if they have lived a full life, we know that despite our grief at their departure they have fulfilled their destiny and that in some sense they exist and will come again. There is dancing and ceremony. Some time after death, and in certain cases at annual events (the Yoruba All Souls' or Halloween), the spirits of certain departed people may revisit the living through the medium of the Egúngún dancer, who wears a mask and a special outfit that completely covers him. The dancer comes to the living and gives messages in a guttural voice. Women and the unqualified are not allowed too close to this dangerously sacred being.

The Gẹ̀lẹ̀dẹ́ Dance-Spectacle

Though like the Egúngún, the Gẹ̀lẹ̀dẹ́ has its elements of mystery, awe, and fear, as a whole it is a joyous and cheerful observance. Far from segregating women and children, it is given primarily in honor of the ancestresses, that they "may be made cool," and children take an enthusiastic part. Here we probably see the Yoruba traditional religion in its totality, its greatest splendor, its most vibrant life.

The event takes place in the market, which is seen as a *limen* (Latin for "doorstep"), a border zone where one passes from one situation to another. Here people meet and goods change hands. Here also the countryside and its people and products encounter the town; agriculture meets commerce. Women dominate the market, just as the spirits of the foremothers in whose line of blood we are, from whose wombs we issued, preside over the ceremonies; the men who dance and sing are but their agents. At night an orchestra mainly of drums gathers, singers and chorus with them. One by one maskers enter, their masks worn on their heads. Ọrọ Ẹfẹ, "the voice of joking" on behalf of the foremothers, lampoons at will and ratifies the norm. The divinities are invoked and honored, Ogún in his virility, Èṣù in his two-facedness and as messenger of the gods. Prayer is made for the special needs and concerns of the people, and always for long life and the gift of children.

During the night ceremonies, the masquerade (the sequence of masks) includes the Spirit of the Ancestresses as Great Mother, white and bearded, as well as Spirit Bird, which has a long, pointed red beak and white feathers. This is "she who killed her husband to obtain rank." These are the aspects of the foremothers we are seeking to cool, to placate. (In the daytime the other aspects are manifest.) The "hyena" appears and heralds the end of the night festival.

On the following afternoon, children begin the dance, practicing the steps and how to carry the masks. The performers become older and more adept. And then come the adults; drums and chorus, costumers and artists combine to produce a spectacle that the Coliseum, the Royal Albert Hall, Carnegie Hall, and the Sydney Opera House cannot rival. Toward the end, a deified ancestress dances, bringing blessing and joy— the other aspect of the mothers' power, the one we want to ensure. Woman is envisaged as playing her part in the Yoruba world under the Supreme God and among the rest of the pantheon.

The Powers of Magic and Charmed Objects

Finally, there are what we may call mysterious powers. It is preferable to emphasize matters like worship, healing, prayer, and the power evoked by music, art, architecture, and sacred location, but for now let us say just a little about magical charms and incantations. They consist of formulae of words used with small objects, which can localize and trigger the power evoked. Here is an example: A husband gets good evidence that another man is cohabiting with his wife. From a doctor he obtains a charmed piece of thin rope or a posy over which incantations have been said. He puts it at the entrance of the woman's bedchamber and stays away. The woman passes over it, and when she and her lover engage in adultery, either he is thrown off and, falling three times, dies; or he will find himself unable to withdraw, so that he and the woman have to call for help and their shameful deed becomes known to all. Such a couple are likely to repent most sincerely for their infidelity. The man pays a compensation and the husband and wife can make a new start. This magic is called *Mágùn*, which appropriately enough means "Do not get on." Similar in effect are the amulets and other protective objects often used to ward off harmful powers. This is a worldwide and ancient usage that the Greeks called *apotropaic;* that is, there is a turning away of something oncoming.

THE YORUBA RELIGIOUS WORLD AS A WHOLE

Other topics in Yoruba religion, such as divination and sacrifice, have been included in Chapter 5, but enough has been said to indicate its main features. In this teaching we have the outline of an obviously impressive corpus or body of religious material. Traditionally, this material was not written down, but in its exactness of form and repetition of the myths, rituals, sayings, and liturgies (set forms of wording and services), it can compare with whole strata of the Bible or the Hindu basic scriptures, the Vedas. Large portions of both of these scriptures were recited and handed down by word of mouth for generations before they were put in writing. In fact, both the Jewish and Hindu traditions long considered writings potentially dangerous, for they could get into the wrong hands and were liable to cause error unless carefully safe-guarded, since copyists could make mistakes and heretical editors make changes. The whole structure of Yoruba thought interrelates in an eminently satisfying fashion. There is also much about it that fits with the best of Islam, Christianity, and Western science. To phrase it another way, there is much that can accommodate these incoming ways of thought to produce a system that is essentially African but is able to withstand new pressure and to grow into the fullness of an emerging world humanity.

One can attempt to explain the manifold complexity of Yoruba religious thought from various points of view. The historian can point out that traditional society was not static and did not lack history. From Yoruba myths and legends, from word study, and from comparing the accounts of Arab or European travellers, we can piece together a history of the various invasions, migrations, and interactions of Yoruba history. The strata of the religion echo these interactions. The social anthropologist can see in this religion a reflection of a social structure in which the various features of the divinities' life mirror life on earth, kingship, family structure, and the relations between towns. A psychologist will see in the religion many images of the human mind at work. Many modern social scientists would see evolutionary processes and the dialectical materialism of class struggle and economic factors. Features of all of these approaches are valuable. In a study as complicated and as subtle as this, no approach can be rejected out of hand. The scholar of the ways of the divine, whether called a divinity student, a theologian, a religionist, or what you will, studies the religious behavior and thought of human beings. But this behavior is itself based on centuries of observation and experimentation by the best minds of the cultures being studied. The Yoruba religious system is the distillation of the highest thought of a brilliant human group. We can join the study of this system to our study of other groups in various parts of the world and go on, if we wish, to link it to our personal observations of things divine as manifested in the human heart and mind and in the cosmos in general.

The Confluence of Islam and Christianity into Yoruba Religion

Later in this book we shall explore the non-African influences upon the Yoruba traditional religion. Here we can be brief. Islam was known for many centuries in Yorubaland, but the traditional religion remained impervious until early in the nineteenth century, when various Muslim theocrats and warriors began to take Yorubaland into account and an emirate was set up at Ilorin. Even so, the traditional religion was resistant. Then, as traditional society became convulsed by civil war and slave trading, people began to respond to Islam. During the time of British colonial ascendancy (the 1890s to 1960), many Yoruba joined Islam, no doubt attracted by its strength and beauty. Some scholars believe that these Yoruba wanted to be members of a world religion, did not like being classed as pagan, and did not want to be Christian. Even so, the traditional religion has deeply influenced Yoruba Islam. Christianity, as we shall see later, penetrated Yorubaland beginning in the 1840s. It was one of the main purveyors of Western education and modernization. At the same time, the sincerity of the Yoruba search for Christ for its own sake cannot be doubted. Yoruba traditional religion has penetrated worldwide churches such as the Roman Catholic, Anglican/Episcopal, Methodist, and Baptist, as well as the bouncing, rollicking, expanding Independent African Churches. African Traditional Religion continues in its own right, practiced in the traditional way as well as in new ways that employ modern principles and organization. It remains very much a living, viable entity well able to use modern life, as it used the old, as its vehicle of expression.

We now turn to the religion of the Akan of Ghana, which is sufficiently like and unlike the Yoruba religion to make comparison worthwhile. Again, our information comes from African thinkers who have pondered the material for centuries and who, during the last century, have added Western learning and languages to their skills.

CHAPTER 2

The Religious World of the Akan of Ghana

The Akan number about five million. They live mainly in the West African country of Ghana (formerly the Gold Coast), where they constitute the largest cultural group (18 percent); some of them also live in the neighboring Ivory Coast. Their country stretches along most of the coast of Ghana, then inland through the forest to the southern reaches of the great West African grasslands. The Greenwich Meridian passes through Accra, the Ghanaian capital.[1]

Dominating the forest zone that stretches northward toward the place from which some of them originally came are the Asante (formerly spelled *Ashanti*), a mighty member of the Akan people with a long history as a powerful kingdom. Their sphere of influence reaches the ocean, and their traditional structure not only survives but is active. They also have the distinction of having hit the Victorian British imperialists spectacularly on the head during their prime a number of times in the last century. Only early in the twentieth century did they lay down their arms. The following account mainly concerns the Asante, but it also applies to their neighbors, the Akwapim Akan in the southeast (who also speak Twi, one of the Kwa languages mentioned above) and the Fante of the coastlands, whose customs and languages are related.

---

[1] Note that this meridian was named "Greenwich" by Eurocentric (English) cartographers; it would be more logical to rename it the "Meridian of Accra."

A ROYAL LADY'S ACCOUNT OF THE AKAN SYSTEM

First we give extracts from the notebooks of the late Evelyn King, an Oxford-trained historian who lived in Gold Coast/Ghana from 1956 to 1962. Her tutor in these sessions was Madam Yaa, by marriage a member of the royal circle in the Asantehene's (king's) court at Kumasi, the ancient capital. They met regularly both at Kumasi, at the house of Dr. Alex Kyerematten, and at Evelyn King's home at Legon, Accra.

Although she was counted as being Asante, Madam Yaa was proudly aware of her family's connection on one side with the area northwest of Kumasi, and on the other with the southeastern towns of Akwapim. She was highly educated in the traditional manner of growing up among ladies who rejoiced in and carefully followed the old ways. She had also been sent daily for study to some English women educators who, having lost their men-folk in World War I, devoted themselves to the service of God in Gold Coast/Ghana. She was a voracious reader, whose knowledge of Western ways of thought, of science in general, was wide and obviously bookish. She had committed great parts of Milton, the prayer book, and the Bible to memory. She loved to illustrate what she was saying by drawing with her stick in the sand in front of her favorite bench. According to Madam Yaa,

When a wife and husband come together in love, the wife will lie on her left side and honor and caress the husband with her right hand. When she gives herself to her husband in ectasy she receives his seed, and the two bloods come together. It is a great climactic moment that seems to involve the whole universe, bringing into oneness so much that is not one. It is obvious that the main giver is the woman, though our menfolk like to talk of woman as a mere mold into which man pours everything. The mother gives the *mogya*, "the blood." This immediately connects the person conceived with the mother and her ancestors, both female and male. The child's descent and inheritance are for us determined through the mother's ancestors in the female line (*abusua*). As our proverb says, "Everyone knows a person's mother."

We can trace a child's ancestors back to the woman who founded the kin, and know the physical and mental characteristics that are being reborn and reshaped in the womb as the child grows. Similarly, the mother's clan inheritance determines the Asante clan to which the child will belong; it gives the child the characteristics, rights, and duties that go with the clan, and in some cases even determines the child's occupation. Wherever the child goes in Akan-land, he or she will have clan members to turn to. A child's months in the womb, when it hears its mother's heartbeat and voice, and is totally one with her, must permanently shape the child.

The mother's religious devotion, her peace of mind, and tranquility of soul all affect the child—as well as what she eats and drinks, and even what she thinks, for there are things a woman must avoid at those times because their spiritual and physical influences may be contrary to those that benefit the child. The woman's body and her food come from earth; the physical constituents she is giving the child come from earth. The mother's regard and reverence for earth is of first and last importance to the child. As our drums say: "O earth, earth, at birth we depend upon you. At death we repose on you. O earth, earth, condolences." For us the earth is not a god (*obosom*), nor is she God; but she is a divine being who has a day and rites of her own. It is not without significance that the last great war of independence against the imperialists, which was also the first step in gaining our independence, was led by a woman and was named after the earth—Asase Yaa, the Thursday-born Earth. She is that which is below, the basis on which the people stand.

On the man's side, when he releases his life power and it flows into his wife to form a child, he gives that child his *sunsum*. This is a hard word to translate because so much of our entire religion and philosophy meets up in it. For the moment let us say "spirit," but as with all philosophical discourse, the same word can have many meanings. The father gives his spirit to the child. He also contributes the child's spirit (his personality), as well as passes on the spirit of the ancestors on the father's side. This nearly always connects the child with the great gods who preside over the *ntoro* (also to be translated "spirit"), of which *sunsum* is itself a manifestation. In the old days, every child was taught to keep up "the washing" of his *ntoro*. This was a reverencing of his patron deity or god (*obosom*). These gods were children of God, rivers, lakes, the sea. As the children of God derive spirit from him, so a child derives spirit from his god's spirit-stuff, as well as characteristics, duties, and privileges.

Besides these inheritances from mother and father, the child is given a spirit- or soul-being by 'Nyame, the Supreme. It is a portion of 'Nyame's own being and is called *'kra*: something in heaven that is dismissed by God to come upon that child, and in some sense the person's fate (*nkrabea*) or destiny. We have a saying, "The child that appears before God to beg his fate, if his fingers are open, will never accumulate money or possessions."

The child also has a mysterious spirit or breath or ghost called *honhom*. To my mind the Christian expression "guardian angel" comes near it in meaning.

Depending on the day on which he or she is born, the child is given a day-name. Each day has its own religious observances and connections, as well as its own place in the great cosmic movements of sun, moon, stars, light, and dark. Accordingly, a child reflects his or her day and does well to be cognizant of the cosmic influences upon his or her innate characteristics.

When we die, the part of the person that came from the earth returns whence it came. It does not perish but is born again in another form, as grass or herb, to nourish other beings; it becomes a constituent of the beloved soil, or part of one of the ever-present insects or of a human. Elements of the spirit-stuff, received from the mother's ancestors, remain (for long or short periods) connected with objects or places associated with the deceased; other elements are reincarnated in new children; some abide with the ancestors. The ancestors are in a sense living in their descendants, present in things associated with themselves but also in their own realm. When we invoke them and pour a libation, we look downward, therefore some say they dwell under the earth. But if I press myself to think where they are or how they live, I can no more finally imagine them as living in a shadow-kingdom below, reflecting our life in the middle, than I can see God as a light-king reflected in his heavenly court above the court at Kumasi.

Other spirits or souls, related to a person's individuality or clan or national personalities and individuality, return whence they came. If someone has a very powerful *sunsum* and has developed his or her divine side, then I suppose that inasmuch as divine things live on, so will that person.

The human being, then, incorporates so much of the divine and spiritual; it is wicked to kill—even in words and thoughts. That is why it is wrong to perform the sex act in any but the most propitious circumstances. That is why it is so important always to keep the correct balance and harmony among the various elements in ourselves.

Additional Commentary

As she spoke, Madam Yaa drew with her stick in the sand; the completed diagram looked like Figure 2.1 (page 24). One should begin at the center, with the dolls that represent the human being (Figure 2.2, page 25), and move outward. Madam Yaa has explained most of the items mentioned, but here are some further explanations.

The stools (thrones) of the ɔmanhene (king) and the ɔhenemmaa (queen mother) indicate the national political and social structure. (See Figure 2.3, page 25.)

Bonsu the whale dwells in Ocean, and epitomizes power and physical size. A strong and big man may be lucky enough to earn the name Bonsu. Songs, dances, and legends preserve the exploits of the great "whales" of Akan lore.

The children of Onyame include the river Tanɔ, who was called by God and did not respond immediately. He was fated to flow through hot savannah lands. The drumbeat says of him:

> The river crosses the road,
> The road crosses the river—
> Which is the older?
> Pure, pure Tanɔ.

The cave in which he rises and his shrines may still be visited with refreshment and delight.

Bosomtwe, another "child of Onyame," is a mysterious crater lake not far from Kumasi. The rafts on the lake have to be propelled by swimmers, not oars or motors. Now and then marsh gas accumulates and explodes, and the god is said to be firing his gunpowder. Everybody born of an Asante father is associated by blood with one or another of these divine protectors and can claim kinship and assistance from others of the group. In another sense this association also means an Asante is related to one of these and thence to God.

Onyame is God over all. Proverbs and titles tell much about God, but

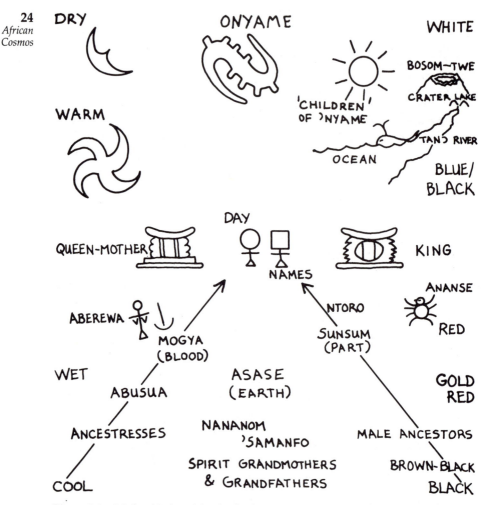

DRY

ONYAME

WHITE

WARM

'CHILDREN' OF ƆNYAME

BOSOM-TWE

CRATER LAKE

TANƆ RIVER

OCEAN

BLUE/ BLACK

DAY

QUEEN-MOTHER

NAMES

KING

ANANSE

ABEREWA

NTORO

SUNSUM (PART)

RED

MOGYA (BLOOD)

WET

ASASE (EARTH)

GOLD RED

ABUSUA

ANCESTRESSES

NANANOM ƆSAMANFO

MALE ANCESTORS

SPIRIT GRANDMOTHERS & GRANDFATHERS

BROWN-BLACK

COOL

BLACK

Figure 2.1   Madam Yaa's writing in the dust.

he is finally unknowable. Though spoken of as "he," this is not to imply that he is male. He is close and always present to help. When lost in a busy airport, one can repeat the *mantram* "It is Onyame, Onyame, who flaps the flies for the tailless cow." Yet there are no shrines or priests for him. He is not personified as a white-haired old man and father figure above the clouds, nor as a shining sun god, though there is a tinge of these things in the thought of many. The nearest analogy in the world of comparative religion is the ineffable Hindu Brahman, as it shades off toward Brahma.

   Below Onyame in the diagram is an *adinkira,* traditional stamped-cloth design signifying *gye 'Nyame,* literally "except Onyame." "Nothing exists—except Onyame." "In the beginning there was nothing, except——,

Figure 2.2 Akuaba "dolls" from Akan country. They can be used to instill ideas of classical human beauty and to induce the spirit of childbirth to come upon the bearer. The iconography has been compared with the Egyptian hieroglyph ankh, "life," "resurrection." The figure with the new-life coiffure has a double-axe motif on the back of her head, perhaps linking her across Yorubaland to the women of ancient Crete. The figures bring together the cross and the circle, the limits of the horizon and the infinite sky. (Photo: Laurie R. King)

Figure 2.3 Mmaadwa, the stool of a female elder. Asante stools are monozylic (carved out of one block of material) and can denote the status of the owner or represent a proverbial saying. When not in use, a stool is kept on its side, lest a wandering spirit take up its abode there and possess the next person to sit on it. (Photo: Laurie R. King)

at the end nothing, except ——." "I fear no one, except ——."[2] The design signifies the omnipresence, omnipotence, timelessness of God. At independence it figured on one of Ghana's first stamps.

Below the crescent moon there is a swastika-like sign that, like the cross, wards off evil; like the Hindu swastika, it brings good luck. It is used in a special festival hairdo for a noble lady's hair braiding. It may go back to the sign of the Siamese twin crocodiles that have two maws and tails but only one stomach. It is a symbol of unity in multiplicity.

The *polaric (warm/cool, dry/wet) and color symbolism* as given by Madam Yaa is probably idiosyncratic to her, but it is a reminder that African thought is at least as subtle and impressive as Taoism on these matters. The scholar has to be on the lookout for the interplay of natural polarities, birth/death, life/the recycling of corruption, left/right, sky/earth, male/female.

Farther down the diagram is *Aberewa, the old woman.* She is, in a sense, the primordial woman. In the myth she is preparing food for her children, and as she pounds her mortar the pestle keeps banging the sky (the word *Onyame* means both "God" and "sky"). Therefore God goes away. To get close to him again, she piles mortar upon mortar and almost reaches the sky. She needs one more and calls to one of her children to give her one from the bottom. When it is removed, the whole tower of mortars tumbles down. Thus it is that the human being, represented here by the woman, seeks its own space and then wants closeness and warmth again.

Ananse the spider has many stories told of him. Once he accumulated all wisdom and stashed it in a calabash on his head. He started to climb a palm tree and lost his hold, and wisdom scattered everywhere. Moral: Bits of wisdom are everywhere. No one, however clever, can monopolize all knowledge. Ananse the spider has crossed the ocean to the Americas: Br'er Rabbit is his avatar on this side of the Atlantic. He is a trickster with inordinate sexual and eating drives. Yet he is in us and controls us all.

Nananom 'samanfo, the spirit grandfathers and grandmothers, are "the ancestors," "the living dead." When an outsider first encounters the Akan cult of the dead, he or she tends to think of the dusty and cobwebby, to feel depressed and morbid. But gradually one's spiritual eyes adjust, and one begins to perceive the love and care of the dead for the living and yet-to-be-born. They live their own life and yet are concerned for our true welfare and the welfare of the unity we form with them. The living have to come to terms with the dead and with death, and this is a time-honored, proven way of doing so. To the person who has lived a good life and done what is right, death is a doorway to the same

---

[2] The dashes represent a pause in speech, a pause that the hearer's thoughts complete.

Figure 2.4 Two Asante gold weights against a kente *cloth (shown about half size). The two men meeting recall a number of proverbs. The friends Adu and Amoako meet after many years: "My, how you've changed!" Or: "You say 'How are you' / But I'm holding my belly in hunger." The small weight on the right has been said to represent time and eternity. (Photo: Laurie R. King)*

honored position. (For a few other Asante proverbs, motifs and spirit-beings, see Figures 2.4 and 2.5.)

POLITICAL AND HISTORICAL BACKGROUND
OF THE AKAN RELIGION

In African thinking, the sciences and other disciplines are not divided; they still intertwine. Much history has already been given in describing the Akan religion, but it is not dates-and-dynasties history or a variation of chronological events. The tense used has been the "anthropological present," yet there has been a time sequence. At this stage of study it would be futile to discuss whether belief in the Supreme God preceded belief in the gods, or whether the notion of the One God evolved from polytheism. One can with greater precision and benefit give the history of the religion during the last two hundred years or so. This has been reconstructed by the historians around the history of the kingdom of the Asante.

The kingdom of the Asante dates back in its present political form to the work of Ɔkɔmfo Anokye and of Osei Tutu in the early eighteenth century. The Akan people at that time were under the rule of Denkira, a region that lay to the southeast. Central to the Asante liberation was the coming of the golden stool. Ɔkɔmfo Anokye caused it to descend

Figure 2.5 Sasabonsam, *the hairy red monster of the Asante forest. Here the monster reflects the "flying fox" of the primeval forest, the crucified Jesus, and the Muslim tradition that devils have horns and that their legs point backward. The carver obviously enjoyed his joke at Christian expense. This work is reminiscent of a second-century Roman graffito depicting a worker adoring his God—a crucified figure with an ass's head. (Photo: Laurie R. King)*

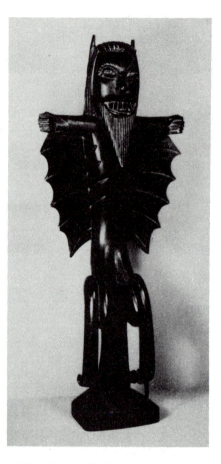

from a cloud onto the lap of the king. The Asante believe that the soul (*sunsum*) of the people is associated with it. It is a palladium and a symbol that has brought together the original groups as well as new-comers; it is more national than tribal, a principle of inclusion as much as exclusion.

The stools of the kings of Asante are kept in a chapel. On the death of the king (Asantehene) his stool is blackened with egg yolk and soot-black and placed in the chapel. His corpse, after suitable treatment, is preserved elsewhere as a skeleton articulated with gold wire. At proper intervals the stools are offered blood, drink, and nourishment. This is a means of calling upon and strengthening the past kings who are now ancestors, so that they may give advice, power, and prosperity to the nation.

The reigning monarch is chosen from among those eligible by reason of, among other things, their matrilineal descent. He is never absolute in power, never a tyrant, but rules within strictly defined rules, preserving the power of every section of the ɔman (nation), from the young warrior bloods to the old women-elders. Especially difficult for a West-

erner to understand is the position of the ɔhenemmaa, somewhat inade-
quately translated "queen mother." This is a woman of the appropriate
matrilineal group, not a spouse or a mother (*genetrix*) of the king, but
one who represents and personifies the women of the kingdom. She is
a monarch in her own right, reverencing her ancestors in office and
offering obeisance in the chapel of the queen mother's stools.

We mentioned the part Ɔkomfo Anokye played in setting up the
confederacy. *Ɔkomfo* is usually translated "prophet." On the one hand,
Ɔkomfo Anokye was a dreamy person, perhaps even subject to bouts of
what might be called epilepsy—like some of the Old Testament and
other major prophets. On the other hand, he was a brilliant statesman
and politician, as astute as Bismarck. The Akan still use *ɔkomfo* for ministers of various deities and for people who can become possessed by
spirit-forces. In some respects the anthropological terms *medium* and
shaman are appropriate.

The king, the queen mother, the elders, the priests and prophets, and
all the people of the nation make up one mystical and corporate unit.
Sometimes the Asante are called "the porcupine" (*Kɔtɔkɔ*). It is also the
name of one of their football teams and is an art motif. The Asante curl
up in a ball and fight off any who attack, for they are one round thing
and no part can be separated from the others. It is an amazingly resilient
system that has survived so much, and in each generation it has adapted
and assimilated. Following the growth of Islam, Muslims were encap-
sulated as a community living parallel with those who followed the
traditional religion. Muslims were employed as accountants, scribes,
traders, ambassadors. In some traditional cults like that of the god Tanɔ,
some features of Islam were assimilated, but no mass movement toward
Islam was permitted. The centers of tradition were carefully preserved
from Muslim influence; thus no circumcised person could become Asantehene. As the influence of Christianity, Western imperialism, and
Western education, science, and technology grew, there was violent
resistance, but over the years there has been spectacularly successful
selective acceptance of these things; there has also evolved an Asante
Christianity that imaginatively uses Western education. Modern African
nationalism posed a problem. Kwame Nkrumah took the title *Osagyefo*,
"Supreme Leader," which had belonged to the kings, but he is gone,
and the Asante are a loyal part of the Republic of Ghana.

COMPARISON OF THE YORUBA AND AKAN SYSTEMS

It is the reader's task to compare, contrast, and juxtapose the Yoruba
and Akan systems, to give what the Germans call *Auseinandersetzung*,
"setting of the one against the other." It would be easy to slip both
systems into the same set of categories and find them very much alike.

But are they? Is Olódùmarè the same as, or just very similar to, On-yame? Are both identical with God and Allah? As for the next rank in the divine hierarchy, are the Òrìṣà very much like the "children of 'Nyame?" Are both of them more like the gods of the Greeks and Romans who ranked below Zeus and Jupiter or like the divine attributes and archangels of Christianity? Is Ilẹ̀ the same as Asase, the Earth? Are the teachings on the ancestors and the lesser powers similar? I believe that in each case differences will be found between the Yoruba and Akan religions, but that the two religions stand together when compared with Christianity and Islam, the religions of the ancient world, or even the religious systems of India, Papua/New Guinea, and Oceania.

CHAPTER 3

The Religious World of the Bantu

The Bantu-speaking peoples dwell in lands that stretch from north of the equator in Nigeria and Mount Cameroon down to the Cape of Good Hope (Africa's Land's End). From there, to the north and east they occupy areas in countries as far afield as Somalia, Kenya, and Uganda. There are about 100 million of these people. Over the centuries, the Indian Ocean, Atlantic, and Nile-Saharan slave trades cost them millions of young men and women in their prime, after which came the decimation caused by colonialism, its new way of life, and its diseases. Most of the Bantu-speaking peoples gained independence from 1960 onward, but in South Africa millions of the most gifted of them are still under alien rule. There the name *Bantu* is almost a term of opprobium, meaning "second-class citizen," but there is no reason to abandon a great word because of its misuse by the white temporary overlords of South Africa.

THE ENIGMA OF THE BANTU LANGUAGES

The discovery and solution of the sphinx-riddle of the Bantu languages is a romance in itself. Roughly, the solution was that the Bantu languages add suffixes, infixes, and other particles to word roots, many of which they hold in common, to formulate meaning. Thus Ki-Swahili,[1] a language that has assimilated some Arabic and English vocabulary over

---

[1] Spelled with a hyphen here to indicate the root, but correctly spelled *Kiswahili*.

the centuries but remains basically Bantu, says for "man" *m-tu*, for "men" *wa-tu*, and for "things" *vi-tu*. To make an abstract noun it uses the prefix *u-*; thus, taking the Arabic root *hur*, "free," it makes *uhuru*, "freedom." Similarly, in Uganda—a Kiswahili word used by the colonists for an arbitrary agglomerate they put together—is the old kingdom of Bu-ganda, the Ganda homeland. In their language, Lu-ganda, the first class of prefixes includes all words for human beings that begin with *mu-* or *ba-*, giving us *o-mu-ntu* "a person," *a-ba-ntu* "people." Other classes give us by similar methods words like *ekintu* "thing," *ebintu* "things" (from the *ki- bi-* class, which includes many things), *omuti* "tree," *emiti* "trees" (from the *mu- mi*-class, which includes trees). There are also classes for place and so forth.

Implications for Religion and Philosophy

Placide Tempels, a Belgian Franciscan working among the Luba in the Congo (now Zaïre), was able to grasp something of the religious and philosophical importance of the linguistic discoveries. In his *Bantu Philosophy*, which appeared soon after World War II in Flemish but did not become widely known until its French editions of the 1950s, he made apparent that the Bantu grasp a notion of basic life, vitalism, essential being, of which all that exists partakes. God, the spirits, human beings, and the natural world are expressions of this at various levels. Tempels's work was not well received by some church authorities because they were afraid of the colonial authorities, some of whom feared it would make the blacks "uppity." Many Africans do not like Tempels's work because it still has the colonialist air of the days when it was written. It speaks of "our mission of civilizing" the Africans. Scholars did not like it because laymen (in this case churchmen) had no business thinking of brilliant ideas before the university scholars did, and besides, Tempels really had not read the literature or studied the proper academic disciplines. Tempels's "ntu-ism" was followed up by French-speaking scholars and writers of the school of *Présence Africaine*, a most important Paris Africanist journal, and by Germans like Janheinz Jahn. The Rwandan priest-philosopher Alexis Kagamé has refined and expanded the basic idea and added much of his own. Perhaps poor Tempels, who had yet to suffer many things at the hands of the authorities and scholars, has his best monument in a small group of African Christians in Shaba (Zaïre) who call themselves *Jamaa*, "the Unity," "the Family." In their daily married lives they try to work out the African ideas to which he was pointing.

The religious significance of this mystery of Bantu "ntu-ism" made manifest has still to be worked out. The amazing achievements of linguists, historians, anthropologists, and students of diseases and blood have shown that the Bantu hypothesis applies not only to words, but to some extent to customs, technology, agriculture, and thought. In traditional Africa, religion is part and parcel of all these things, nor are religion or philosophy or medicine or technology separate.

Our best academic guides tell us that the Bantu peoples migrated across Africa from one original area and then outward from a few secondary centers. From study of the history of languages and from archaeology we can get some idea of where they picked up technologies like iron making, certain cattle keeping methods, or certain musical instruments, as well as social customs like the formation of age sets. Certain common words belong to the oldest basic stock, which the German called *Ur-bantu*, the original, primordial language, or to its first embodiments as we know them in actual use. Then if we study reliable texts concerning the religion, strategically drawn from various parts of the Bantu world, we find a number of common beliefs and customs, some of them connected with certain word roots. In effect we have a good understanding of the underlying substratum of religion in this enormous area.

The Beautiful Names of God and an "Avoidance" Word

Following the example of their Muslim brothers, the Bantu can contemplate the Names of God. Among very many Bantu people, God is called *Mungu* (in Swahili), or words like it, such as *Mrungu* (among the Digo), *Umlungu* (among the Nyika), *Mulungu* (among the Yao). An analysis of the usages justifies scholars in thinking that *Mulungu* and its cognates are "a summation of the divine." Although God is connected with the heavens, the word seems also connected through the primordial root with the spirits of the dead who dwell below. Godhead partakes of their nature and they of its. The deity's names and titles—*Modimo/Molimo, Leza, Immana, Unkulunkulu, Ruhanga*—are all widespread and have deep meanings indicating its almighty power, omniscience, creatorship, its accumulation of ages. This kind of study is valuable not only in regard to the names of God but also in regard to religious practices. A word like Kiswahili *mwiko*, translated "taboo," "an avoidance," can again be traced in its root forms from East Africa across to Southwest Africa to very ancient religious antecedents.

Millet, the Primordial Grain

Millet is the oldest cereal used by the Bantu. They have adopted many other commodities, and for some of them, as with the "Nilotic" River-Lakes peoples, cattle have become the "ultimate concern." For the Baganda, perhaps the banana is more "ultimate" than most things. Even so, millet remains for many of the Bantu a symbol of life and fertility, its hairs deeply aligned with the hirsuteness that comes with puberty, its beer with religious celebration (not to mention nourishment and vitamins). This is not to say that the Bantu think their ancestors set these traditions, customs, and usages up to make them (the people) what they are, but that the words they used and the things they did indicate the kind of people they were. This is the mold which formed them and their descendants, however much newer and outside things may shape that which is above the substratum.

THE RELIGION OF THE GANDA PEOPLE

In studying the Bantu systems we may take as our paradigm the religious system of the Ganda. The Ganda have a rich indigenous tradition of history and literature, both oral and written, which goes back a long way. In addition, it has been written about for more than a century in English, and this makes it accessible to readers all over the world. The Ganda are a patrilineal people of about two million. They live on the eastern shore of the mighty central African lake called Lake Victoria by its nineteenth century "discoverers" looking for the sources of the Nile. The area where they live is mainly plateau country, at 4000 to 5000 feet, with good rainfall. As this area is on the equator, the climate remains much the same most of the year. The country's richness in plants, trees, animals, and insects exceeds imagination. One patch of primeval forest may have more species of birds and butterflies than the whole of Britain, one sector of land more varieties of mammals than all of Europe.

The Myth of Kintu

We may begin our study of the Ganda with the story of Kintu. (Our Gandan teachers ask us to note the elements *Ki*, "thing" and *ntu*, "being"—hence "thing-person.") The story still exists in Ugandan oral tradition, so we asked our students in the university at Makerere in Uganda to collect versions from their grandmothers! I also gave them mimeographed copies of the earliest printed accounts, along with accounts collected by colleagues who are experts in oral history. The story in its many forms runs roughly like this.

> Kintu came with a cow into our land and there met Nnambi, who was from the sky. Nnambi wished to marry him, so her father Ggulu (the Sky) got Kintu's cow stolen and brought it to his abode. Kintu followed, Ggulu tested him, and Kintu proved himself. So he was granted his wife and they were given millet, bananas, cows, chickens, and goats. The father warned them to get away before her brother Walumbe (Death) came back. After they had gone some way, Nnambi, though she knew the consequences, insisted on going back for the millet they had forgotten. Walumbe therefore accompanied his sister on her return. When Nnambi and Kintu had children, Walumbe wanted one of them as a servant. The couple refused. They had more children, and again Walumbe asked. He was refused, so he began to kill the children. Kintu went to Ggulu to complain about this, and Ggulu sent another son to try to kidnap the killer, but Walumbe escaped.

There are various versions of the final line of the myth. In all of them,
Kintu has to accept death as the poignant fate of the human being, as something that comes with marriage and procreation.

We have to relate the story to its context in the literature, that is, in the type of material of which it is an example. It is a typical Ganda story-with-a-moral, a kind of cross between a myth, a "just-so" story, and an Aesop's fable. It tells us how Ganda civilization began, how death came, and how humanity and humanness survived death. The price of humanity and culture is death. In the broader context of African thought, the myth fits with many stories about the coming of death. Naturally, many Christian Ganda relate it to the Genesis story in the Bible, and it is not difficult to use it as background to the Christian story of the Son of God who was sent to overcome death by rising from the dead, as well as to humankind's search for full humanity and eternal life.

The Ganda Divinities

After studying the Kintu myth, we turn to a study of the divinities, the *Balubaale*, who so dominate Ganda religion as viewed from outside that the first missionaries called the religion Lubalism, from the singular *lubaale*. Some of these divinities were men or heroes who were promoted to be gods (the Greeks did this too; it was called *euhemerism*). Some are natural features like rivers or waterfalls. One of these is Ssezibwa, the waterfall. When the students and I went to visit her, the canoe men asked if any of us were circumcised, for this divinity hates such people (as indeed traditional Ganda elders still do) and overturns boats carrying any. Any who confessed were "bumped."

Here is the story of another divinity—Kibuuka, the Ganda Mars or Samson:

> A huge, mighty warrior from the Ssese Islands, Kibuuka came ashore with one leap to help the Ganda against the Nyoro [their close neighbors and perpetual enemies to the northwest]. From a cloud he rained missiles on the enemy and every day they were routed. One day the Ganda captured much booty, including a beautiful Nyoro maiden, who was given to Kibuuka. In bed at night he told her his secret. Within a day her kinsmen ignored all else on the battlefield to project spears and arrows into the cloud that was hovering over the battlefield. Kibuuka fell mortally wounded into a great tree. His scrotum, testes, phallus, and other relics were preserved in a shrine through which his spirit could be called upon to give strength and advice during the wars against the Nyoro.

In Uganda, students can visit the tree, which stands by a road; the relics are in the Uganda museum. During the civil wars in the 1890s the Ganda religious factions destroyed Kibuuka's chapel and took the rich offerings there, but the bundle containing the relics was given to a missionary, who sent it to England. The British queen gave it back to Uganda at independence.

Figure 3.1 A "fetish" or locus of a wilderness spirit from Buganda. It consists of two bead-decorated lions' claws mounted on strips of cob (deer) skin; they are kept in two concave baskets wrapped in a long strip of bark cloth, which serves as an insulating material. In a third basket offerings are made as the devotee approaches the inner sanctum. (Photo: Laurie R. King)

Another *lubaale* is Ddungu, who is the spirit of the wild. His main shrine had a drum containing earth, leaves, herbs, and skins of the different animals a hunter hopes to bag. Ddungu's medium will advise where game are to be found. If a hunter guided by Ddungu goes out in the dawn and comes upon a woman, he must turn back. As old Ganda people say, "Hunter's blood has to do with death; it is sharp. A woman's blood has to do with life; it is round—and is finally more powerful." (See Figures 3.1 and 3.2.)

Many of the *Balubaale* are connected with the Great Lake, which at the point between mainland Buganda and the Ssese Islands is called *Nnalubaale*, "the womb of the gods." Mukasa, the god of the lake, is the Ganda Neptune; he is in certain circles recognized as the greatest of the gods. Others consider the greatest to be Muwanga, who is leader of the *Balubaale*. It is something of a conundrum therefore that the creator God, Katonda, whom the Muslims and then the Christians accepted as the equivalent of Allah and God, is sometimes referred to as a *lubaale*. This is made more perplexing by the apparent lack of attention given to him in the old cult as well as by the vagueness of his image. Clearly, like other Bantu people the Ganda had a strong belief in a sky-deity who was separate and above others: Ggulu in the story of Kintu signifies "Sky" or "Heaven." Maybe the Ganda people do not consider it neces-

Figure 3.2 Another Ganda spirit-locus. The mummified umbilical cords of twins are wrapped in bark cloth and decorated with cowries. This can become the tabernacle of a spirit of womanly fertility. (Photo: Laurie R. King)

sary to distinguish clearly between *Balubaale* and other categories of the divine.

The Spirits of Lineage, Locality, and Ancestors

The next category to which we turn are the *Misambwa*, the tutelary deities connected with a lineage or a locality. A large rock or a panther can be their seat. They might be spirits of dead clan members who adhere to the jawbones of those buried in the clan cemeteries, which are so deeply feared and reverenced. There are also the *Mizimu* (the Bantu word root here is very old and widespread), the ancestral ghosts, who greatly influence life and must be placated and nourished.

Storage Cells for Spirit-Power, and the Cult of Royalty

The study of Ganda religion includes certain objects in which spirit-power is stored by practitioners—animal horns and other containers that are used to perform certain tasks. The Ganda also possessed a cult of kingship connected with the Kabaka and the royal women; it can rank for its metaphysical completeness and its hold on the mind of the people with the cult of the traditional Japanese emperor. The religious aspects of Ganda customs regarding birth, marriage, and death are also of great interest, but these and many other issues must be left to the reader to follow up, using the suggestions for further reading as a guide.

Some Arguments among Traditionalists and Historians about Ganda Religion

Ganda religion is deeply interesting in the way it has evoked arguments among its own traditionalists and among Western-style historians and theologians, both native-born and foreign. Historians of religion have been remarkably fecund in suggesting relative chronologies and comparative sequences for the various components of Ganda religion. Their colleagues cannot agree, but have put forth modifications and countersuggestions. Some allege that Katonda, the creator or demiurge, was a comparatively insignificant *lubaale* until Islam picked him out as the equivalent of Allah and then Christianity took him over as God. Yet he has many of the characteristics of a "High God," a "Deus otiosus" of the type the older anthropologists loved. This indicates that he was there from the beginning, but it is unlikely that we shall ever know for sure. Again, tradition says that the cult of the *Balubaale* came over from the Ssese Islands during the reign of the sixteenth Kabaka. Tradition also says that during a darkening of the sun, Kabaka Jjuko called them over. We know how many generations ago he reigned and roughly how many years to allow per generation. There was a major eclipse of the sun on the equator in the seventeenth century, and this could be the event indicated. Other scholars see this one piece of tradition as slender evidence to weigh against the major part of the tradition, which makes the *Balubaale* primal. However, if they are new, then basic Ganda religion has to do with spirits of the clans and with the ancestors. The other systems were added later.

Let me mention one last historical puzzle of this kind. The cult of the Kabaka, from the early nineteenth century (if not much earlier) until it was destroyed by the government of Dr. Milton Obote in 1966, was central to the Ganda religion. It is also clear from tradition that as a kingship the Ganda is junior to the kingship of Bunyoro-Kitara to the northwest. That kingship itself is traced by myth and legend to "Nilotic" tribes migrating along the Nile and the lakes and to mysterious heroes called the Bachwezi, who performed their mighty deeds and disappeared into the earth. The upshot of this excursion into precontact history (that is, the time before the Arabs and Europeans came in the 1840s and 1860s) is the notion that an African religion is made up of variable components interacting in various ways and in varying proportions. The history and social structure reflect and interpret components of the interaction, but the religion is a living whole in the minds and lives of the people. African traditionalists have never lacked critical and historical notions, but their purposes often differ from those of modern Western scholars. Often we warp tradition if we insist on asking such questions as, "Which is anterior; which of the versions tells the true facts?" We can see the cult of the Kabakas gaining prominence as the kings of Ganda established central power and especially when they got muskets and gunpowder. But the Kabaka's mystique never destroys that of the clan heads and ancestors. All the components interact and find a balance.

Later on in this book we will consider the meeting of the Ganda traditional religion with Islam, Christianity, and the modern world. Again we shall see the same pattern: The different components meet and interact; only as a result of drastic intervention, like the ending of the Kabakaship in 1966, is any single component removed. Even Christianity, Islam, and modern Western science, technology, and thought in their turn were woven into the web of Ganda tradition. Presumably, there will come a time when the modern world will finally break the web. But people were saying that about Hinduism and Judaism a century ago, and those religions live on.

THE RELIGION OF THE "SWAHILI"

As the twin of the Ganda religion in our study of the traditional religion of the Bantu, we may take the beliefs and practices of the people who live along the central coast of Tanzania. In the 1890s, a great East African thinker, Sheikh Mtoro bin Mwinyi Bakari, wrote down for the instruction of the incoming German colonialists a collection of statements about the traditions of the "Wa-Swahili" (*Desturi za Waswahili*). Writing in the Arabic script, he defined the Swahili people as the folk living on the coast from Lamu, near Malindi in northern Kenya, to Lindi in southern Tanganyika (which after union with Zanzibar was called Tanzania). This is his technical definition and we follow it here, without implying that today there is a people called Swahili. The material he gave has its greatest applicability to the people living between Tanga in the north of Tanzania and Lindi in the south; it also applies to their neighbors, whom he names: the Digo, the Segeju, the Zigula, the Bondei, the Doe, the Zaramo, and the Yao. The following are extracts from notes on conversations regarding this Swahili classic with some of the elders of the town of Bagamayo, which is the center on which Bwana Mtoro based his work. Until the Germans built up Dar-es-Salaam it was the capital of the sultan of Zanzibar's mainland dominions and the caravan center from which the great safari routes radiated out as far as Zaïre and Uganda. It has been for centuries a crossroads for invasion and trade.

In Bwana Mtoro's day the area was agricultural. The greater rains fall from March to May, the lesser from October to December, with a pronounced dry, colder season from June to September. The land is well watered in places, and some rice can be grown. Mainly it is scrubland, with hills on one side and the coast on the other. The main crops are millet, maize, beans, yams, and manioc. Indian hemp and tobacco are fairly easy to grow, and on the coast there are coconut groves and fishing. Chickens and goats scavenge and browse everywhere. Kiswahili is very widely used, but the other languages are still common, all of them belonging to the Bantu classification. Most of the peoples concerned were originally matrilineal. It is impossible to give an accurate estimate of the population, as the area is large and sparsely populated, but there are perhaps one-half to one million people.

Bwana Mtoro's material is chosen because of the large area it concerns and because of its coverage of different peoples. It also provides considerable chronological depth, whereas most of the other material uses the "anthropological present." Again, the thinking of an African writing at the beginning of the colonial period about his people's traditional religion is hard to find. Bwana Mtoro and my teachers in Bagamoyo were highly educated in the manner of the old Qur'anic schools, but they were also deeply versed in the life, traditions, and customs of their African background. The two exist side by side in a kind of double helix of practice and thought. Where they collide, the Islamic takes preference, but mostly they live in symbiosis and pass one another at different levels. This makes it possible to discern the Islamic and arrive at the African, even as a metallurgist can often separate one metal from an amalgam. Later on we shall take up the Islamic side of the material.

Distinguishing the Traditional African from the Islamic

My teachers were at first a little bewildered by this business of picking out African traditional religion. So far as they are concerned, things offensive to Islamic principles have been eliminated, and the rest—where it is not specifically laid down by Qur'an, *sunna* (tradition) of the prophet, or by the books of law—is just general custom. Also, while they are conscious that something Indian or European is foreign and that something Swahili is the homegrown, organic product, the concept of Africanness is comparatively recent. For them and Bwana Mtoro before them, things from "upcountry," from inland, that have to do with the tribes of the hinterland, are -*shenzi*—that is, almost uncouth, savage, or pagan in the Latin sense. They think easily in terms of what is *dini* (revealed religion), *sunna* (the tradition of the prophet), and *mila* (custom). This last most nearly approximates what we mean by African traditional religion.

Bwana Mtoro and the others speak often of Allah and use the Bantu *Mungu* completely interchangeably with it. But the center of their thoughts is the human being, the child becoming female and male, the life as woman and man, from birth, through puberty, marriage, work, and adulthood to death and the afterlife. Next, their interest is in the things that disturb the harmony and completeness of human life—diseases and spirits. Somewhere in the background, mentioned regularly and considered important, but not given formal explanation, are the shades of the ancestors.

41
The Religious World of the Bantu

The Stages by Which a Boy Becomes a Man

Mtoro clearly describes the different stages in the life of a male child, though Islamic elements have taken the place of some traditional lore and modified the rites. For instance, in the boys' initiation no beer is brewed. The boys are sent to the camp (*kumbi*) when five to seven years old. To Mtoro the initiation is not just an adolescent premarriage rite, and not only an infancy custom like scarification, indicating identification with a tribal group, but part of discipline and education, part of being made fully a male human being. The Islamic idea of ritual cleanliness and the Western notion of imagined hygiene are easily fitted in. But above all there emerges the idea that the boys are no longer just members of the families into which they were born, but brothers to one another, alumni of the same graduation. For the mixed "tribal" population around Bagamoyo, the rites were valuable in producing oneness.

Mtoro says that the people begin initiation by sweeping the graves of the *wazee*—"the old ones," the ancestors and ancestresses. They sweep and weed them, offer perfumes and incense, and pray: "We come to you, our old ones, we bring you your child and grandchild, God (Mungu) grant him health. You have died but your shades (*vivuli*) are alive (*vizima*). May he be not sick. . . . When he recovers, we will come and sweep again." It is not only that ancestors lacking attention can send illness, but initiation is a time of perilous exposure, and witchcraft and sorcery can wreak havoc. Ancestral support strengthens the spirit of the novices.

Then the people celebrate the *manyago* dances. According to the etymology, this is to do with the loins, the genitals; that is, it includes instruction in sexuality. The peoples toward the south, in connection with similar dances, make likenesses to frighten and instruct, masks to cover the face or the whole body. Small statues of wood and of clay are carved or shaped and used to illustrate and teach proverbs and wise sayings, even the sex act (see Figures 3.3 and 3.4). The teachings are related to appropriate dances. The dancers take on the personalities of spirits, the spirit of lion, of pig, of fire, of other spirits, especially evil ones. In modern times, the colonial official could figure as one of these.

Women and the uninitiated are excluded. A boy to be initiated is called *mwari* (maiden), perhaps, says one theory, because the men's rites may be derived from the women's to compensate males for having nothing spectacular like the menarche and the power to bear babies. The initiates are segregated naked in the *kumbi* (secret hut) in the bush. It is built in the old circular fashion and perhaps symbolizes the womb. The whole symbolizes rebirth. The first boy is brought out, then held on a board. The operator twiddles the boy's penis around and then cuts

Figure 3.3 Pepo *figure. The Makonde
of East Africa (Tanzania and Mozambique) who have settled among the "Wa-
swahili" have developed the art of the
visual aids of their initiation camps into
new forms that can be sold to tourists.
Their* pepo *figures of spirits are especially intriguing. Here is one spirit becoming two—by fission rather than by
generation. It is by a master carver who
lived at Bagamoyo. He said, "The wood
told me what it was and my tools revealed
this* pepo." *The striated finish is a con-
vention for indicating a spirit-being. The
figure perhaps illustrates the proverb
"Evil thoughts, like spirits, proliferate
speedily"—in other words, control such
thoughts before they grow. (Photo: Laurie
R. King)*

with his knife. The pain when the inner skin is cut is intense, but the
boys are expected to show courage, especially where circumcision has
been added to adolescent initiations that are mainly tests of endurance
and manhood.

During convalescence the boys are not allowed clothes, coverings, or
a fire. It is very cold at night, and insects torment the boys by day.
During this whole time the boys are taught wisdom and discipline,
mainly through songs and the recitation of proverbs. The experience
must be like brainwashing, with the initiates deprogrammed from the
past and reprogrammed for the future. The classical elements in initiation, the segregation, the "in-between" time, and the reintegration into
society, are clearly brought out by Bwana Mtoro. The return to the village and to the celebration and gift giving, coming after the misery of
the camp, must leave a permanent mark on the boys' minds as they
settle into the interminable monotony of everyday adult male life, a
monotony all men must accept.

A Girl Emerges into Womanhood

In dealing with the customs in the life of a girl growing up, Mtoro is
very concise, but it is possible to augment his terse remarks from oral
tradition and from classical Swahili poetry, a fair part of which seems to
have been written by women. A female child is called *kigori* from the
age of seven onward, and when around thirteen she menstruates she is
called *mwari.* If her menstruation is delayed, she is given a doll to carry
and takes it wherever she goes. The type of doll mentioned by Mtoro is
one made of pieces of gourd, and it is usually regarded as female. It is

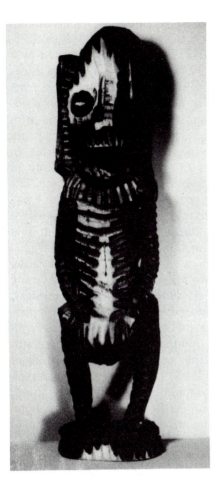

Figure 3.4 Makonde sheitani figure. This carving goes beyond the traditional world of the African pepo (spirit) toward the Islamic sheitani (Satan) figure. Note the likeness to sasabonsam (Fig. 2.5). (Photo: Laurie R. King)

probably only for brevity's sake that he does not mention the male counterpart, made of wood. Possibly, as perhaps with the Akan dolls of Ghana, the doll is an archetypal child-image, for to many minds the bearing of children is a mystery, terrifying but immensely powerful.

Mtoro says that at menarche the *kungwi* is called, and she imparts to the girl-become-a-woman the meaning of what is happening, the correct way to use and dispose of napkins, and the method of deodorizing and perfuming herself. She gives her the belt of beads she must always wear as a dignified and proper woman. Mtoro often mentions the *kungwi*. Not the mother, she is the young woman's sponsor, her tutor in initiation, her "best woman" in marriage, her coach and midwife in childbirth, the one who ratifies her divorce and, if she is still alive, guides her through menopause and onward toward death. Unfortunately it is impossible to establish exactly how the *kungwi* is chosen. In my informant's mind, the *kungwi* was somehow representative of womanhood. If the girl is already promised in marriage, perhaps the *kungwi* is chosen from the woman-kin of the future husband, otherwise from women closely related to the girl's father. If this is a general rule, it is possible that the *kungwi* is the matron "reverend and discreet" appointed by a male-dominated society to continue the power of the male ancestors and their present embodiments. On the other hand, the *kungwi* seems always to stand against the husband, by whom she must be mollified, propitiated, and compensated. She seems rather to represent the principle of the ancestresses. Also, if the *pepo* (spirit-possession) rites are initiations, the *kungwi* is analogous to the *mganga* (doctor, shaman). In those ceremonies the *mganga* initiates the candidate into a group of people who are recognized to have and control a spirit-power, *pepo*. The *kungwi*, like the *mganga*, has a whole group of people whom she has initiated and who must obey her summons to come out and help with a novice. So the *kungwi* signals the reception of the girl into the group that has and controls the power of womanhood, a spirit-power.

It appears that up to the calling of the *kungwi* not much formal instruction has been imparted, though living with older sisters and young women relatives would hardly have left menstruation a total mystery. The giving of instruction follows the onset of physical maturity. Emphasis is placed on the potentialities womanhood implies, the basic, ultimate, and exclusive means of passing on human life; woman's strength in society and among her sisters and her power to conserve, initiate, attract, and command are also emphasized. The responsibilities associated with her power are not to be forgotten either. Menstrual blood, akin to blood at childbirth, is seen by my African teachers to be antagonistic to the powers of the hunt and of war. The power to create human life is such that it can interfere with some aspects of male spirit and with the efficacy of ritual and religious observance.

Mtoro briefly mentions the seclusion, the "enclaustration"—that is, the shutting up of the girl, which could last in the old days from the onset of menstruation to the giving in marriage. Some scholars see in this the time when male domination was imprinted on the mind of the young woman. Others say that older women, looking back on a married life of continuous childbirth and toil in the fields, thought of it as a blissful time of leisure during which, though growing pale from not going out in the sun, they grew fat from plenty of food. For these good people, fat is beautiful. *Unene na uzuri, kitu moja:* "Fatness and beauty are one thing," says the proverb.

When the time with the *kungwi* is over, the parents are told that the young woman should go to the *muyombo* tree for the celebration. This is the bark cloth tree (*Brachystegia*). It is dark brown in color and gives excellent shade. Its bark used to be hammered out to make a most pleasant-smelling cloth, which is still associated with things old and sacred. The color brown is linked with the redness of blood and hence menstruation. If the girl's *kungwi* followed general practice, the beads around the hips were white, indicating purity. The third elemental color of the Bantu world, black, may be conspicuous by its absence. It is associated with hair, including pubic hair, and the neophytes are usually shaven.

Bwana Mtoro says that at the *unyago* dance, the celebration, the girl is taught to vibrate her buttocks and practice other positions, and she is given many riddles, many of them of a sexual nature. Eventually she is taken to the tree. Beer is drunk and songs are sung. New clothes and jewelry are distributed, and at evening the new women come into the village. They parade, receiving gifts for some days, then normal life is resumed.

Marriage, Islamic and Traditional

In marriage, the Islamic *mahari*, the bridal guarantee, easily overlaps in meaning with the bridal compensations of African traditional religion, where strength and wealth are given to the bride's group as recompense for losing her power and potential in the human ultimate, the ability to reproduce. The contract, the solemnization, and the Islamic side are given in full by Mtoro. In the African traditional religion part, on arrival at the bridal chamber the *kungwi* gives the groom his wife, after he has paid suitable compensation. Again, only after the *kungwi* has purified him by washing and receiving another fee does she allow him to approach the bride.

Mtoro says that the *kungwi* arranges that the bride is a virgin. She checks beforehand; if there is no hymen (this can be the case for any number of reasons), she puts some chicken blood on the cloth of virginity that she places under the bride and shows off to prove that the bridegroom is the first. Variations of this technique are found in many cultures. It was mainly the Victorian middle class that took it literally. The principles behind the desire for virginity are so old that it is difficult at this time to discuss them with either traditionalists or Westerners. The latter get angry, ask why men are never supposed to be virgins, and remark that men merely do not easily take to fathering other men's children; they like to be sure that at least the first child is theirs, as much as it is obviously the mother's. After a generation or two this debate may resume more fruitfully.

If the man is impotent, the *watani*, the "joking relations" of African tradition who appear most prominently at marriages and funerals but are always goading people toward their duties by their gibes and pranks, pour scorn on him. Crushed, he has to free his wife for another man. The principle for thousands of years has been that if there is no sexual intercourse, and therefore no procreation, there is no marriage. It is only in our own day that this has been questioned, making it possible at last for religious principle to free itself and not be a mere handmaiden to tradition. One may question whether religion's basic principle for marriage, love, depends on physical features like a woman's hymen. Most Western people today believe that it doesn't. One may ask as well

whether it depends on a scared young man's ability to perform immediately and vigorously.

Cosmology

Bwana Mtoro writes at length about spirit-dances, mediums, possession, "exorcisms," and shamans. This material will be analyzed in a
special section, along with the material on witchcraft, sorcery, and
charms. Mtoro's work also includes a brief but valuable section on Swahili cosmology. Since the people of East Africa had contact across the
Indian Ocean with Arabia, India, and beyond to Indonesia and China
from ancient times, and since Islam has incorporated much Indian
Ocean lore into its own folklore and substratum of thought, the task of
distinguishing the specifically African and Bantu is not easy. Here is an
attempt.

In the original cosmology of the people speaking Bantu languages,
inhabited lands interspersed with wilderness stretch endlessly to the
ocean. The wilderness is not evil and not something to be overcome;
she exists and has an important place. In some ways she may be nega-
tive, but spiritual mysteries, new life, virgin land, and renewal, as well
as important foods, come thence. Beyond the ocean are other lands, but
the land as a whole is surrounded by endless ocean. Above are the
heavens; below are the earth and the dwelling place of the ancestors
and of certain spirits. The earth is the mother who gives life, and in
death the people return to her. Fire and water are below, as thunder and
rain are above. The sun and moon, stars and planets dwell in the sky
and have their seasons. Their life and the life of the people are one. The
sun goes down from sight and, travelling where it cannot be seen, rises
each morning. The course of the moon is like a woman's. Sometimes
the moon is said to be swallowed by a snake, and when the peoples of
the world tell the snake that all love the moon, the snake vomits her
out. The sun, the winds, and the clouds make the dry and the wet.

The Swahili, like other Africans, knew nothing of clocks, but they
know the seasons and the times for doing things. A close examination
of the tense structures of the Swahili and other Bantu languages has led
some scholars to believe that the Swahili and other Bantu-language people of East Africa have a better grasp of the fullness of seasonal time
than of chronological time. The present is intense and loaded by the
weight of the immediate past. The near future is vivid. Beyond that,
time rolls on but is not clearly envisaged.

The Swahili Religion in Its Historical Context

Western scholars have been able to trace vestiges of a Swahili language back to the ninth century. There is evidence of a literature written
in Arabic script going back for some centuries. Oral tradition indicates
that Swahili language, culture, and religion have been deeply influenced

by and related to coastal Arabic language and Muslim culture for at least three centuries.

We know from the history of the Bantu migrations into East and Central Africa, from Bantu meetings with older inhabitants, and from non-Bantu migrations that the cult of the ancestors, certain features of witchcraft and sorcery, and certain uses of the lesser powers are very ancient. The *pepo* spirit cult probably came next. The non-Muslim parts of the boys' initiation and most of the girls' initiation seem to be comparative latecomers, taken over from non-Bantu tribes migrating in from the north. Islam, especially since the 1840s, when the sultans of Zanzibar took a deeper interest in this part of Africa, has affected every feature of Swahili life. In fact, it had done so to such an extent that the Christian missionaries working on the language from the middle of the nineteenth century onward saw themselves as rescuing the language from Islam.

The Coexistence of African Tradition and Islam

German and British colonial administrators often seemed to assume that all Swahili were Muslim. But deep down, African traditional religion continued in easy coexistence with Islam. Sheikh Mtoro bin Mwinyi Bakari's work on the customs of the Swahili, which we have referred to, was written in the 1890s and concerned the state of affairs before the massive German occupation. In it Mtoro makes clear that the Islam of the Swahili is of a high quality. The law of Islam is well known and kept, the Qur'an is studied, the pillars of the faith are accepted, and the five duties of Islam are performed.

Nonetheless, at each one of life's turning points (the rites of passage) there are parallel ceremonies, the Islamic and the African traditional. For instance, at marriage the bridegroom and a representative of the bride meet before the proper Muslim official, draw up a contract, and give and receive a "dowry." Soon afterward the bridegroom has to go to the bridal bower amidst the singing of traditional and very un-Islamic songs and go through various traditional ceremonies, ending up with gifts to the *kungwi*, the tutor, who presided over the bride's initiation and her womanhood. The *kungwi* eventually gives him his bride. That night he has to prove his manhood and she her virginity, in keeping with tradition, and if a divorce or annulment results, both a Muslim and a traditional process will be carried out. Another striking example is in the case of barrenness or difficulty in childbirth, when both the Muslim official—with his Islamic readings, potions, and remedies—and the *mganga*, the African doctor, will be called in.

In the case of the Swahili, it is clear that an African traditional religion can survive intact under Islam. From the point of view of the historian of religion, the Swahili case is remarkable in that African traditional religion survived not only in conjunction with Islam but in its own right. A number of members of the tribal groups mentioned as comprising the

Swahili by Sheikh Mtoro did not become Muslim. Of these some came into contact with Christian missions, both Roman Catholic and Anglican, which took the view that African traditional religion must not be destroyed but fulfilled. (In recent years these missions have also refused to try to steal converts from Islam.) The outcome was that Christian clergymen learned all they could about African culture and custom and tried, with advice from traditional elders, to preserve the best in it and to use it to make Christianity truly indigenous.

The Swahili present a unique means of studying the relationship of a language to a people and to their religion. The basic Bantu matrix and the central controlling thought-forms came out of the minds and traditions of the ancestors and ancestresses. These thought-forms embodied in words molded, and were molded by, the subsequent generations of the people, as well as by people who came from other tribes; they were then molded by Arabs with Islam and by Europeans with Christianity and "modernization." Yet the center and heart remain African and traditional. This topic is still in the early stages of research.

In the new Tanzanian nation, Swahili has become the national language. Everything traditional and African is given its due place; Christianity and Islam both flourish. The modern world, socialism, technology, and science are also welcome, but the welcome is on African terms. This is a way of adapting to the coming world of the twenty-first century, a way that human beings who do not know themselves or their roots may envy.

CHAPTER 4

The Religion of the "Luo" River-Lake Peoples

The term *Luo* refers primarily to language, but there is much more than language that links "Luo" people of central Africa to those of eastern Africa. They have common oral histories of their migration. From the traditions of their northern groups—the Shilluk, Nuer, and Dinka in the modern Republic of the Sudan—the scholar can follow the wanderings of the migrant ancestors along the Nile. These people joined the Acholi of Uganda and continued with the southern "Luo" in Kenya, moving along the Great Lake and into Tanzania. (The habit of scholars was to label them *Nilotic,* but this term is under heavy fire, and a replacement for it has not yet been found.) Over these thousands of miles, affinities in civilization, language, and way of life exist along with similarities of religious thought (quite apart from the ever-present mystique surrounding cattle, grass, and river that permeates the very existence of the river-lake peoples). Recent research makes it possible even to imagine that this kinship of culture and religion could be extended to the Maasai and related peoples whose habitat stretches from the great Rift Valley down to the Indian Ocean. These are the people who have caught the world's attention by their fearlessness in facing lions or machine guns while protected only by spears, red ocher paint, and leather shields.

Scholars studying remotest African antiquity also point out that the river-lake people of central and eastern Africa may owe a great deal to a civilization that straddled Africa when the climate was wetter. From southeast to northwest, across the widest part of the continent, there was a series of connected, habitable lands by the shores of a great chain of lakes and rivers. The humans who built up their ways of life—fishing, boating, growing crops, and keeping cattle—have left remains by the former lakes and rivers which the archaeologists working in the present-day deserts of the far northwest hope to decipher. Here and there habitation has been continuous, and the people living in these areas have retained traces of that great former widespread culture in their religion and customs. The "Luo" peoples we are studying are part of a great heritage that may prove even more grandiose than we would have imagined.

The religions we are about to study act as a keystone to the arch of African religion we have tried to build in previous pages. The "tribes" before us have attracted devoted European students, and above all have produced their own indigenous scholars who can translate the wisdom of the elders into the terms of Western learning.

THE RELIGION OF THE DINKA PEOPLE

The Dinka number about one million and inhabit about 150,000 square miles, from Rejaf on the White Nile eastward past Wau, toward the Bahr el Ghazal (5° to 10° north latitude, 27° to 32° east longitude). Their neighbors are the Nuer and the Shilluk. Traditionally they had incredibly little besides cattle, religion, and customs to pass on from one generation to another. Materially they lived in the barest, harshest simplicity, but their religion indicates a harmony with the cosmos, a fullness of life and development of intellect that are not easy to rival.

In part we will follow the account of the Oxford scholar Godfrey Lienhardt, whose work is to this day accepted by the Dinka as bearing correct witness to the teaching of the elders. Lienhardt acknowledges, besides his debts to the Dinka, how much he owes to Evans-Pritchard, who will always be known as one of the greatest geniuses of our century, and who learned his trade in this same part of Africa. Both men built on the work of a long line of Austrian, Italian, and other European and American missionary scholars, as well as on the findings of British administrators who worked in the area despite incredible difficulties during the previous century. Before Dr. Lienhardt's material was canonized in Dinka-land, it was discussed in detail with English-speaking Dinka students who as refugees had found their way to Makerere College and Mukono Seminary at Kampala in Uganda. In a number of cases their accounts differ from Dr. Lienhardt's, but it is impressive how well his findings have stood up to detailed study and criticism. The writings of Dr. Francis Mading Deng, a Dinka who has studied at Khartoum, in Britain, and in the United States, are now available and sustain the main lines of Lienhardt's account.

The Dinka World of Divinities and Spirit-Power

The Dinka seem to think of things in three concentric circles of ideas. The widest is *jok* (plural *jaak*), which may be translated "power," "spirit." Within this group are *yeeth* (collective form; singular *yath*). These include divinities of the clans or the descent groups. Then there are divinities, which Dr. Lienhardt calls "free-divinities"; they have associations with individuals and hence with their families. The most frequently heard word of religious connotation is *Nhialic*, a locative (that is, having to do with place) meaning "in the up, above," hence "in the Heavenlies." *Nhialic* creates, *Nhialic* provides. Often it is used in the same way the expression "the Lord above" is used by Jews or Christians. Dr. Lienhardt translates it "Divinity." According to Dinka myth,

> *Nhialic* (Divinity, "In-the-above") and things below were together. "In-the-above" granted us one grain of millet a day and this was sufficient. But woman wanted more for her loved ones, and her hoe [or perhaps it was her pestle] poked "In-the-above," who withdrew. Then death and the need to work came upon us.

A second myth tells:

> The human [we] was pushed back and forth in the darkness by "In-the-above," who at first refused to let the human see more and then gave the human an axe. With it the human hewed out a separation from "In-the-above." Light appeared. Then "In-the-above" gave the human a way in which to move, and as the human moved, hit the human on the head with a barbed spear. One ingenious person covered his or her head with a stone, and when "In-the-above" blunted his weapon on the stone, the human escaped to reproduce.

These myths imply some basic ideas about the human and "In-the-above." It is very good for the two to be close, but the closeness is an undifferentiation like dark before dawn, like life in the womb, like boys and girls before puberty. "In-the-above," as we see him, appears purposeless and cruel, but this causes some of us to grow up. Life in a confined space, with little to live on, is all very well; but people with initiative, especially women, the great innovators, desire more.

The picture-background of the first myth is the Dinka woman tending her millet garden with her long hoe or pounding her mortar. As important and romantic as man's work is—tending the cattle and thinking about the divine—the digging and hoeing of the earth and the preparation of food make culture possible. The picture-background of the second myth is the traditional fish-trap or dam in the murky waters of the river. The fish is alive and well but can hardly move; when a way is opened it darts forward, only to be hit on the head. But the ones that get through are the cleverest, the quickest, and the most experienced—or the luckiest—and they reproduce.

The Divinities of the Forefront

Apart from this prominence in myth, "In-the-above" is continually mentioned in invocation, prayer, and conversation. He/she/it seems ever present in the back of the Dinka mind; however, those divine beings whom Lienhardt calls "the free-divinities" appear to impinge much more frequently on daily and seasonal life. The "free-divinity" Deng is so important in Dinka thought that some earlier European students of this religion confused Deng with Nhialic, the one "In-the-above." Others identified this power with rain, for *deng* is also the Dinka word for rain. Thunder is the club with which he strikes; his favorite sacrificial ox is black and white, with colors and markings like lightning flashing across a dark sky. He is connected with procreation just as the rains bring the grass, the source of life. Deng also possesses prophets; he can make his will known through them and empower them to lead his children, the Dinka, against foreigners who threaten them. Though Deng can be identified in some sense with Nhialic, the Supreme, Deng can also be a *yath*, the tutelary spirit of a clan group, a "totemic" spirit as the older anthropologists would put it.

Macardit is another whom Lienhardt classifies as a "free-divinity." He is "the great black one" who everyone hopes will go away. In general the divine is just and reasonable; the inexplicable blind cruelty of life, the sudden endings to joy and contentment are the work of Macardit. Sacrifices to him are the inauspicious black kine, offered by a son who is neither the first nor last, in the compound of a nonsenior wife, as near as possible to the bushland. If Macardit possesses a person, the person may become sterile, so people do their best to refuse him. His "mounts" (the people he possesses) are quite often older women.

The "free-divinity" Abuk is female. Her name is the same as that of the primordial woman, and she may be that lady elevated into divinity. Sometimes she is spoken of as the wife or mother of Deng or of other divinities. In general she presides over womanly activities, especially the growing of millet and the brewing of beer therefrom. She does not possess people, but among some Dinka she is associated with the waters of the river and with the little water snakes.

The Mystique of the Sacred Cow

Other powers are also active in Dinka religious thought. The names of spirit-powers and their activities, above all in sickness and death, assume great prominence, but the daily and perennial Dinka essential interest is cattle. It is the cattle whose needs for grass and water dictate movement, but beyond this human beings identify with their cattle, and a young man will in imagination reflect his whole life onto the display-ox given to him at his initiation. When asked how he can identify with an animal castrated when young, the answer is that castration has made the ox grow fat and beautiful and think not of cows but of its human counterpart. The outsider has to hold his peace, despite the fact that so few Dinka are other than long and lean, and male performance is a great virtue. A young man will go to immense trouble to train the horns of his ox, and often the resultant horn shapes are reminiscent of the same custom among the ancient Egyptians. In the dance and in conversation, young men become one with their oxen. Most of the wars among the Dinka and their neighbors go back to arguments over cattle rather than over women or land. As the myth says, God created cattle along with humans. Buffalo and cow were close relatives. One day the human killed their offspring, so buffalo and cow resolved that buffalo would kill man in the wilderness and cow would live with him, to cause him to kill himself or be the cow's slave.

THE RELIGION OF THE ACHOLI

With the Dinka traditional religion we may compare that of the Acholi, who migrated hundreds of miles farther up the Nile than the Dinka and settled along the lakes and streams of north central Uganda. (The correct spelling is *Acoli*, but the pronunciation and literary use both make me succumb to the old spelling.)

The Concept of *Jok*

In keeping with the teaching of Acholi scholars, the generic term on which we focus our study is *jok*, "spirit" or "power." The concept of *jok* may be studied in connection with three *jok* manifestations. The first is *jok pa rwot*, "spirit power located in or near the seat of rulership," "the shrine of the *jok* of chiefdom." These are located in each chiefdom and connected with a stretch of riverside, a hill, or a tree. The natural features are not *jok*; nor is *jok* a sprite dwelling in the natural feature. I went once to what I took to be Baka and Alela, twin hills, male and female, connected with the chiefdom *jok* of Patiko. I was able to look into a most fear-inspiring cave. Though I did not see a mighty snake or a leopard, I felt certain that the *jok* was nearby, and I was glad to retreat to the road. The people who lead one to the cave tell of how at an annual festival in the dry season much beer was brewed and a red and white goat, a red chicken, and dried termites mashed in shea butter were offered. The deity sent a deer, which gave itself up to capture and death. The officiant descended into the cave hard upon the portions offered to the spirit and brought out sand from the cave floor. Various supplications were made, especially by those whose penises or breasts were too small or who could not get children.

Jok is also manifest in connection with a known ancestor of a clan or familial group. An animal or plant or bird may be associated with the group, but it is not the spirit of this creature that is associated with the *jok*, but the spirit of the ancestor, of the lineage as summed up in him. In former days every homestead had its lineage shrine, *abila*. In its center was a small hut often made of slabs of stone. This was the house of the spirit. Near it branches and saplings from certain trees and bushes were placed for standing up spears or hanging up pieces of animals sacrificed or killed in the hunt. In some places placentas of children born in the homestead and, long ago, twins entombed alive in a pot were buried there.

When a shrine was consecrated, an *ajwaka* (diviner, priest) led singing and dancing and then called the ancestors to be present. They would come and speak through her or him. The most recently dead person would tell of his discomfort in the land of the departed, at having no shrine of his own until now. More senior ancestors would complain of the neglect of their shrines, or ask after family members not present. Living members gathered there would make requests and ask advice just as they would of other members of the family. There were other occasions when a shrine would be cleaned and sacrifice offered, often with much beer drinking, dancing, and transaction of family business. In one dance, the men carried the spears back from the shrine while the women doused the spears with water. The spears symbolize the piercing of enemies and predatory animals. In Acholi thought they also represent the penis, which is cooled in continuing the lineage. When there was much illness, ceremonies for driving away evil took place at the shrine. In one such ceremony, a black goat was led in. The elders spat upon it and young men drove it so far away that it would not get back to the homestead.

Misfortune *Jok* and the Doctor's Visit

In addition to the manifestations of *jok* in chiefdom and family shrines, *jok* is manifest in the spirit warfare the Acholi carry on with certain *jogi* (the plural) that bring catastrophe, bad luck, and especially illness, and are not connected with any of the spirits so far described. When a practitioner diagnosed a patient at his or her clinic as suffering from some *jok* illness of this kind, she or he would agree to visit the patient at home. The doctor would don the proper robes and headdress and come with the appropriate retinue of nurses and consultants. After suitable greeting and welcome by an older woman relative of the patient, they would be led in. The patient would be led three times around a stool and seated thereon. Then he would be given an appropriate potion and his body and clothes put in order for treatment. The doctor would sing *jok* songs one after another, and the attendants and the family would join in. Drums and rattle-gourds would beat out the various rhythms. Sometimes the *jok* caused the doctor to shake unbearably all over, so that he or she would signal for the séance to stop. Perhaps the doctor would have to withdraw to bring in someone with more experience, seniority, or strength, especially if the patient just went limp and the *jok* gave no clues as to its nature.

Usually the *jok* was flattered by the attention it was receiving and would give its praise-name, thereby showing itself friendly and willing to cooperate. Perhaps an arrangement would be made with it and it would continue to dwell in the patient and be available for consultation—given the right invocations and rhythms. If the spirit was violent and obviously malevolent, the doctor was in for a life-and-death struggle in an inner intensive care room. Those outside would hear sounds of the treatment, and occasionally the doctor, with gore or other signs of the struggle, would emerge to give a brief bulletin. Then he would return to the work of healing, ultimately destroying and removing the malignancy. Its remains were brought out in a receptacle, usually a gourd, which was then buried deep in a living termite hill or otherwise actively disposed of.

The Fateful Triplets

Besides *jok*, Acholi scholars find that there are three terms often on the lips of the Acholi; some scholars thought they referred to attributes or "children" of the Supreme Being. The terms are *Woko, Wi-lobo,* and *Rupiny.* A woman reaching old age childless would sing:

> I am perched on a treetop like a sparrow
> Like a monkey in a tree
> Alas! Wi-lobo has kneeled on me.

A man about to die without offspring sings:

> Wi-lobo, whose child can I entrust with a task?
> Woko's purpose is to insult me.

Wi-lobo comes from the preposition *wi*, "above, on," and *lobo*, from the word for earth or soil. It refers to one's fate or condition as long as one is above ground, alive. Similarly, *Woko* means "outside"—outside the womb or the grave. *Rupiny* refers to the day-spring[1] when darkness goes and the everyday hazards and pains of life begin. One can do no more about these awful triplets than the Norsemen could do about the weird sisters who spun human fate.

THE EMERGENCE OF THE DINKA AND ACHOLI RELIGIONS INTO THE MODERN WORLD

The river-lake peoples seem to have developed their balanced and complete religion and way of life very long ago. One can imagine this religion and way of life going on and on, round and round like a great ball of riverweed in the *sudd*, the great marsh of the Ugandan Nile that forms as the river meets waters from the direction of Lake Chad and runoff from Ethiopia. Migrations made no great difference to the people as

---

[1]*Day-spring* is a term referring to the first light before dawn.

long as rivers, meadows, and lakes were available and no pestilence or fly destroyed the cattle. The people and cattle took the divine with them. In some cases they carried a little earth or other token from the homeland, but new shrines were set up as they went, and the ceremonies and healings reenacted. (This is all reminiscent of the wanderings of the patriarchs and matriarchs in the Book of Genesis.)

The Balance of Primal Ecology Shattered

As we shall see later in this book, in the first part of the last century the old way of life was rudely affronted as slave-raiders from Khartoum and then imperialists in the service of the Khedives of Egypt came up the River Nile and across the lakes. (The Khedives were a family of Albanian adventurers, originally in the Turkish service, who took over the rule of Egypt.) Nile weed and biting insects that had protected the children of the Nile from outsiders yielded to the steamboat, the beginnings of modern medicine, and the crazy determination of modern man to conquer everything lest he should have to subjugate himself. The peoples of the Nile, such as the Dinka and Acholi, put up an incredibly effective resistance. They made lousy slaves and they drove their cattle out of reach of the attackers. Then Khedival imperialism collapsed, and in the Khartoum area a Muslim Mahdi (Messiah) broke the line of communication with the Mediterranean. After the defeat of the Mahdi, the British took over the whole of the White Nile basin, including Uganda. In the southern Sudan and northwestern Uganda they gave full rein to the idea of the noble savage, a primitive but decent human being who must be protected from filthy outside influences.

The British did their best to keep out outside influences, but Roman Catholic missionaries from Italy and Austria had been serving and dying there long before the British arrival. British Anglican and Presbyterian societies were also allowed to start work. Eventually some American missionaries also came. Then suddenly in 1956 the British abruptly left the Sudan. The northern Sudan, which was almost completely Muslim, took over the government and the southern tribes rose in revolt. After nearly twenty years of civil war during which the south had not been overcome, a means of settlement was found. Recently Muslim law was imposed on the whole country; the outcome of so much struggle is yet to be seen.

The Acholi, who were across the border in what we today call Uganda, suffered the effects of the slave and cattle raids up the river, Khedival imperialism, and the Mahdi's interregnum to a somewhat lesser extent than their kin farther down the river, but suffer they did. Under British rule they received similar treatment, but the Christian missions had much more success because of the leadership provided by a number of outstanding Acholi who were converted, and because of the Acholi willingness to use the school system launched by the missions with government help. When Uganda became independent there were men and a few women from the Ugandan river-lake people able to represent them in the new democracy. Having received a Western education, p'Bitek Okot achieved world renown as a writer. Dr. Milton Obote is from Lango—a river-lake peoples area—and Janani Luwum, who became archbishop of Uganda and was martyred by Amin, was also from the river-lake peoples. When the government of Milton Obote was overthrown by Idi Amin, the Muslim minority in Uganda received the doubtful support of military men whose ancestors had been converted to Islam, and Amin began a reign of terror against the Acholi and Langi. When Amin was finally driven out, Dr. Obote's government was reinstated by the Tanzanian army.

In both southern Sudan and northern Uganda history tended to cast Islam in the role of enemy to such river-lake peoples as the Dinka and Acholi. A good number of both peoples had become Christian, and the type of Christianity that developed among them (both Catholic and Protestant) had been deeply understanding and friendly toward traditional religion. Christianity had also become associated with education and with making one's own way in the modern world while retaining the best from the traditional.

Despite the warnings of the ecologists the *sudd*, the great Nile marsh, is being drained. "Development" continues apace. (The modern world, hating nomadic wandering, loves to tie people down, clothe them, and put them in the stocks of the modern school desk.) Although Islamic law has been imposed in the Sudan, the traditional religion survives in very many ways, not least in and through Sudani and Ugandan Christianity. We shall fill out the picture later on in this book.

The Emergence of a Paradigm of Study

We have now set before the reader three major systems of African religious thought, West African, East African, and Luo River-Lake. As we study them and approach them in their many differences, we see their oneness emerging. Their central feature is the place of man and woman in a spirit-filled cosmos. Each system has its own point of departure and difference of proportion, but some common elements emerge. It is legitimate to use these elements as a paradigm, a system of thought and discussion, as long as we do not try to impose it as an iron framework that distorts the data, the given facts of the living organisms we are studying. We must guard against too facilely seeing a unity and then inventing phenomena to fill up our framework. With cautious steps we can retrace the paradigm that has been worked out for the study of African religions:

—the human being and the ancestors

—the lesser and greater spirits

—teachings about God

—"the faceless powers," sorcery, magic, certain prayers, blessings, curses

—fellowship with the spirit, prayer, mysticism, divination, sacrifice, rituals—especially those of life's turning points

It would have led to a good deal of repetition if we had dealt in detail with these last two—"the faceless powers" and spiritual fellowship—under each of the systems outlined. The following chapter takes up these themes.

CHAPTER 5

Communicating with the Divine: Prayer, Fellowship, and Sacrifice

The divine communicates with the human and the human with the divine: This is a basic tenet of religion. In this continual two-way traffic the divine can speak directly or through intermediary people and things. The direct method is mysticism; one aspect of the indirect method is sacrifice. To these we now turn.

AFRICAN ADORATION OF DIVINITY

The most common form of African fellowship with the divine is bodied forth in the mother of the African family waking before dawn and silently saluting the great spirits of the cosmos and the ancestors of her own and her husband's lineages (see Figure 5.1). She waits upon them in silent communion. I have seen this in an old woman of the agricultural caste of Ankole in upper Uganda. She was a woman who personified the best in that romantic concept we have of the peasant, the person close to the soil and to the realities of life and death.

In most parts of Africa the old man or woman who has lived a full life spends more and more time alone with the emblems (icons) of the ancestors, meditating upon the ancestors, their teaching, their way of life, and their descendants, taking care to think no evil of the living lest the living-dead punish them with illness or accident. I once had the privilege of sitting long hours with such a man in northern Ghana by the Upper Volta border, and later with another on Mount Masaba overlooking the great sweep of the Nile and its marshes toward the Sudan. These people are true mystics who have undergone their own disci-

Figure 5.1   Old woman before the ancestors. Bantu wood carving. (Drawing by Kenneth C. Orrett)

plines and slow years of learning. They have much to teach us all, but few of them have been studied. Words do not convey the meaning of their teachings.

SPIRIT-POSSESSION, DRUMMING, AND DANCING

The most spectacular public and continent-wide example of the direct contact between the human and the divine is the possession dance. It leads easily into spirit-mediumship, where the possessed person becomes an intermediary, though even here the worshippers consider this direct speech from the divine, the very words and actions of the gods. In the Yoruba part of Nigeria this method of worship can be seen quite commonly. Amid dancing, drumming, and the carrying of carved objects dedicated to the divinities, head coverings, masks, and staves, the deity will descend upon a devotee. As the spirit comes down and mounts the worshipper, she or he will gasp ecstatically and go limp, then suddenly leap into tremendous activity and take on the characteristics of the spirit. If it is Ṣàngó, the thunderer, the possessed will be hot tempered, jerky in movement, flaring out in anger. If it is Yemọja, the female spirit of the river, the possessed will take on the great, calm, sweeping characteristics of that Mighty One. People may ask questions of the possessed and receive answers in the name of the divine. These are possessions by the great spirits; God the Almighty does not usually possess in this way. Possession by the great spirits is also well known in Akan religion, where old national shrines have pots and basins dedicated to the gods and on certain days certain people belonging to particular lineages become possessed. These people are not only devotees, but spirit-mediums being used as mouthpieces of the divine. Among the Dinka, Deng especially possesses "prophets," and indeed any Dinka may suddenly be possessed. The Dinka associate a peculiar movement of the muscles with possession by the divinity Flesh. The muscular movements down the back of the neck and the weakening of the lower limbs that one sometimes experiences at hearing a certain cadence of the Qur'an, or in a Christian service when a certain peal of the organ or bells or the sonorous words of a great liturgy boom forth, may be comparable phenomena.

Among the Ganda, there are many shrines at which possession takes place. Some of these are for the major spirits, the *Balubaale*. Near Kampala is a large and neatly laid out compound, at the center of which is a large, traditionally thatched chamber. Young people being initiated into the cult, musicians, and officials have their houses in the compound. On certain days séances are held. The chief medium, a woman wearing the ancient dress—bark cloth—with many beads and other decorations, takes up her presiding position. The orchestra plays (the word *orchestra* is not used lightly or unadvisedly): drums, xylophones, stringed instruments, and reeds are carefully and intricately manipulated. Everyone claps and joins in at appropriate places. Various sacramental symbols of the gods who may vouchsafe to come upon the gathering are laid out, and medical orderlies and retainers stand ready.

A heavy, steady rhythm and the eager longing of the body of worshippers make everything suitable for the coming of a truly great one. A woman becomes possessed and goes forward to squat in the position Gandan women adopt before a superior. Then, crouching and taking up a paddle, she rows around the floor on her haunches as if in a canoe. The Lord Mukasa, the god of the Great Lake, has come. The woman sinks to rest and we may ask questions. Faced with this chance to ask God a fundamental question, I ask the one basic to my subject. "What did his Lordship think of the new divinities coming in, Christianity and Islam?" Mukasa replies: "People who are devoted to me may follow me. Those who follow Katonda [the Creator], whatever they may call him, follow Katonda."

Other questions are asked, but gradually Mukasa seems to lose interest; the medium slumps and is carried out to sleep. The clapping, playing, and singing start again. There is screaming and a boy begins to jump, like some wild animal, all four feet off the ground. He would fall heavily as these jumps increase in height, but the attendants catch him and restrain his leaping. They remove him and apparently succeed in calming him. (I learned later that a passing lesser spirit, perhaps of a suicide or an impersonal spirit evoked and left at large by a necromancer, had taken over the young man. It was drawn out by forcing him to drink an infusion of emetic herbs kept for the purpose.)

Possession by these lesser spirits is a study in itself. Among the Swahili people of the Mrima coast in Tanzania, there is a class of spirit called *pepo*. These are not ancestral spirits; nor do they have to do with the higher spirits. The word *pepo* is an old Bantu word, but it does not have the usual Bantu prefixes—that is, it is not person or tree or thing or place. The *pepo*, though they have many human characteristics, are not really anthropomorphic, though many European scholars have tried to represent them so. And they are not like the jinns and devils of West Asian folklore, though some Muslim scholars have tried to represent them so. Let us analyze a *pepo* dance (*ngoma*) at Bagamoyo, not far from the Tanzanian capital, Dar-es-Salaam. (*Pepo* dances are also easily found in Mombasa, the great port and tourist attraction of Kenya.)

The venue is usually a large *banda*, a large room with a good roof. It has partial side walls that allow easy entrance and exit and plenty of ventilation, while providing an area of shelter from rain and sun. If possible, it is located toward the edge of the town, with outlet toward the fields and the bush beyond, as well as to the beach and ocean.

The person in charge is the *mganga*. The meaning of the very widespread Bantu root is "putter-together, healer." The usual English translation was "witch doctor," which is hardly appropriate. In some senses *shaman*, "master/mistress of spirits," from the Tungus of Arctic Siberia is appropriate. This person is also called the *fundi*, "the practitioner, the expert, the craftsperson."

Cult phenomena like that of the *pepo* spirits occur across the continent. In Ethiopia they are known as *zar*, in Hausaland in northern Nigeria as *bori*. Scholars have explanations that cover parts of the phenomena. One need not be an M.D. to recognize that many of the patients are suffering from physical diseases ranging from malnutrition to anorexia. And one need not be a psychiatrist to detect psychological symptoms and recognize in some of the *pepo* the bodying forth of things that lurk dimly in the human mind until activated or released by association or circumstance. Again, some social scientists will rightly detect factors like the class struggle or the search for status or the coming of new economic systems. Others will perceive the struggle of women who have recently experienced change of status because of the coming of Islam or the influence of the modern West. Having allowed that these things are all possible, is it too much to ask scholars in various disciplines to allow that the spirits have some reality in themselves, so that we may at least begin by not treating our informants as lunatics?

Disembodied human spirits can possess a living person. The best example I ever witnessed occurred once when I was overtaken by evening and the rise of the new moon at the jawbone shrine of a dead Gandan Kabaka (king). I had become entranced, sitting on the sweet-smelling mat, with my back to the high-arching grass roof, gazing at the metal regalia that composed a reredos to screen off the sanctuary. I had not noticed the drummers begin to drum and the dead king's living court creep in like shadows, do obeisance flat on their faces, and then sit on their legs placed sideways. There was a twittering and peeping, and a spirit-wife became possessed. She began to speak in the voice of a man. The other women ululated, the musicians playing the evening salutation followed by the salutation of heroes. I slipped out and crept away, only partly out of reverence and fear of offending, only partly out of fear of getting beaten up. The dead Kabaka's spirit was much too strong for me, and I was afraid: I am always terrified of spiritual rape.

At Larteh in Ghana, one may consult the spirit of a dead person in much less spine-tingling circumstances. One Tuesday I was with a group from the University of Ghana as we visited the house of the bonesetter spirit. There, with invocation, a chicken's limb is broken in exactly the same place as that of a human sufferer; then both bones are tended and set. Both heal at the same time. We went on to the shrine of the Prophetess. Our escort from the edge of the ward was the secretary himself, a University of Ghana colleague. The orchestra and choir were already assembled, the prophetess—powdered in white, wrapped in white, and holding a broom and a stick—had gone through all preliminaries. (These spirits keep better time than Westerners: My guests from Harvard, Princeton, Scotland, and New Zealand had caused us to be late!) I presented my bottles of schnapps. (Since Dutch and Brandenburg times the spirits really prefer this type of gin.) The spokesman poured a great libation—not much liquid, but mighty fine words. It was a mixture of Guan, the old autochthonous language, and Twi:

Spirits of the above, come, drink.
Spirits of earth, come, drink.
Ancestors, spirit grandfathers,
  —spirit grandmothers, come and drink.
Remember the needs of those travelling,
  —those in childbirth
  —those under compulsion
  —those in need of money
  —in need of children.

I found it deeply moving, and prayed silently.

The prophetess danced as the orchestra played, and we all sang. The head drummer was inspired, and his work alone was worth the cost of

Figure 5.2 Dance, trance, and spirit-possession in northern Asante. (Photos by Captain R. S. Rattray in 1922; reproduced by permission of Pitt Rivers Museum, Oxford)

the gin. The secretary whispered that the next invocation would be to the gods of the town. It was rumored that the spirit of the lady possessor was that of a woman who had died giving birth to simultaneous twins. Earlier her father had tried to compel her to marry a man she did not like. Various people posed their questions and made their supplications, and the spirits spoke to them. Much later, the exhausted prophetess was carried out and we, only a little less worn out, dispersed. (See Figure 5.2.)

I trust the reader will forgive a word of warning. It is better not to believe in spirits than to dabble with them, play the fool, or try to use them. Without proper precautions, supervision, and instruction, they are dangerous to humans.

THE MYSTERY OF SACRIFICE

Ritual sacrifice is also something any observant person will see performed all over Africa. Perhaps it will be the breaking of a hen's egg against the base of a tree or the use of a sheep's blood to propitiate the soul of a statue in the Ghanaian capital. Perhaps in the Sudan it will be the offering of an ox; perhaps it will be the decapitation of a dog in honor of Ogun in Lagos, the capital of Nigeria, or a chicken or two in Kumasi in Ghana or Kinsasha in Zaïre, or a goat in a home lot in Soweto, near Johannesburg. (See Figures 5.3 and 5.4.) Let me not be condemned for painting Africa in sacrificial blood. The Victorian propagandists' favorite ploy was to accuse Africans of human sacrifice, in order to excuse their soldiers for going in with machine guns and modern weapons against people armed with spears and bows and arrows, to "free" cities like Benin, Abomey, and Kumasi from such abominations. True, some human sacrifices were offered, many of them to turn back the atrocious interference of the white men. These were few, however, compared with the number killed by European bullets, diseases, famines, and forced labor. Sacrifice is an ugly thing in many of its aspects, but it will not go away even if we ignore it. It can be transmuted and made to bring blessing, or it can remain unsanctified and uncontrolled to wreak havoc among us. (An outsider who comes as an adult to Europe and the United States may be not altogether mistaken in detecting son-sacrifice in war memorials. This is not difficult to document from the German and English hymns sung before war memorials on Armistice and Veterans' Days.)

Sacrifice, in its ritual or ceremonial use, means "a making sacred, an offering that becomes divinized." Whatever is sacrificed crosses over from us to the divine. Basically, human intent and thought are offered in sacrifice. The intent is conveyed and sealed in words and action: They, with any material objects—animal or vegetable—constitute the

Figure 5.3   A Nuer ox sacrificed by suffocation. (Photo taken by Sir E. E. Evans-Pritchard about 1935; reproduced by permission of the Pitt Rivers Museum, Oxford)

sacrifice. Thus a cow slaughtered in sacrifice is not only the sacrifice. Potentially it symbolizes the whole action and content, from the resolve of the offerer to offer, onward to the effect on the remotest bystander who, by seeing and hearing, is associated with the sacrifice. (Even wider consequences are possible: Someone living in San Francisco can be associated by an offerer with a sacrifice performed on Mount Longonoth in Kenya, and thereby involved in its consequences.) Scholars have now collected details of so many sacrificial rites and analyzed them so carefully that we have means of scholarly and scientific exegesis; that is, we can read the meaning of a sacrifice just as we read the meaning of a great text.

The Gisu Sacrifices in Uganda

We may take as an example a type of sacrifice I attended in 1962, 1964, and 1966, near Buwalase in the Gisu district on Mount Masaba in Uganda. (See Figure 5.5.) From the anthropological point of view, the sacrifice is embedded in a rite of passage, the circumcision rite by which a boy passes into manhood. On the day of the circumcision, at the twilight of dawn as objects begin to take shape, the people gather, reciting stylized accounts of how the world began and the ancestors came to that place. They slowly gather at the living-enclosure of the

Figure 5.4 An Asante craftsman sacrifices a chicken over his tools. (Photo taken by Captain R. S. Rattray about 1922; reproduced by permission of the Pitt Rivers Museum, Oxford)

relative of the initiate who is organizing the occasion. The father of each boy (often they can be as old as eighteen, for some fathers prefer to put this off as long as possible) brings a goat. He places his hand upon it. The sacrificer kills it, and the entrails are consulted for omens. The grandfather takes parts of the stomach lining (chyme) and smears the novice. Then the novice is smeared with yeast of finger millet, which is kept by the center pole of his mother's hut.

The boys are then muddied in a watery hollow associated with the ancestors. Dancing, they go to the place of circumcision. As they go forward to the trellis in front of which they will stand, they strike its left post hard with their sticks; then they put the sticks across their shoulders and gaze ahead without flinching. As the outer skin is cut a great cry from all around goes up. The operator does the same to all the

Figure 5.5 Gisu male initiation rites. These are held every two years on the Uganda slopes of Mount Masaba (Elgon). The first three pictures show an initiate after the sacrifice and dancing, taking his stance, and being shown the knife; the final two show his triumph, and his supporting relatives when all is honorably completed. (Photos: Horst Bürkle)

candidates there, then returns to finish cutting the inner skin and the trimming of the first. The boys stand without showing any emotion; then, when told the operation is over, they dance on the remains and dance away amid congratulations. They are now given the cooked meat of the sacrifice to eat. While they have been undergoing the operation, their mothers have been miming childbirth, holding onto the center poles of their huts. When the young man heals and is reintegrated into society, he is given more goats from his father's herd, a share of his father's land, banana spikes to plant, and spears. Before long he gets a wife.

The sacrifice comes at a time when the novice is neither child nor man. He has left the community and the amorphousness of childhood, but he is not yet a man. The rivalry between the older man and the younger is at its acutest and most unresolved. The father takes of the best that he owns, associates himself with it, and gives it to be killed. From its inmost part chyme is taken to anoint and strengthen the boy. Despite the rivalry and loneliness, there is love and blessing and association. The anointing aligns the goat and the boy, and the circumcision is a ritual echo of the sacrifice. A part is offered on behalf of the whole. The male ancestors associated with the muddying are made propitious. The sacrifice takes place at dawn, and may be associated on a cosmic level with the remaking of humanity as at creation and the primordial entry into the land. The mother's act also indicates birth after the blow of leaving the womb.

Janani Luwum, who afterwards became archbishop of Uganda and was killed by Amin, was present one year. He was most anxious to assure Christian Gisu that the Church approved of the rites as long as only God was worshipped. He laughed good-naturedly at my exegesis and remarked that perhaps some of the elements I had mentioned were in the minds of the Gisu; perhaps at some point all of them had come into the minds of Gisu people, but he doubted that all were there at one time. I told him that the great anthropologist Dr. Victor Turner was witnessing the rites farther over the mountain, and I had no doubt that anything I could see in the rites would be only a fraction of his exegesis.

"WITCHCRAFT"

I have placed fellowship with the divine, sacrifice, and the descent of the spirit at the heart of African religion. What of witchcraft, fetish, and juju? Silly use and emphasis of the words is offensive to many Africans, but to many Westerners they are central to African religion. *Juju* was a pidgin word used in some parts of the west coast to refer to the whole of "native superstition." It can be dismissed at once.

Witchcraft is a worldwide phenomenon; so similar are its basic characteristics, wherever we meet it, that witchcraft may well belong to those few human forms of thought and practice that existed before the human race spread out from Africa. Mainly foreigners have studied and written about African witchcraft. It has been easy to import overtones from European and New England witch crazes, and too easy to link African phenomena with nonnative fiends and devils. Foreigners who thought they were bringing good health and enlightenment gave too much prominence to something that, although always present, had only recently grown to epidemic proportions as a result of the European intrusion that shattered the normal balance and happiness of African life. Syphilis, with its mysterious comings and goings and terrible, slow-moving disfigurements; tuberculosis, with its relentless destruction of lungs; and the inexplicable wasting away of children demanded some explanation. In addition there was the misery accompanying the dislocation of African society and economies caused by foreign occupation. The basis of witchcraft lies in human malice and the wreaking of havoc by certain people involved with mysterious dark powers that lurk in our universe. The proposition that African religion and Western science spring from the same roots in the human mind seems at its most attractive here. Both are based on observation, trial and error, and the creation of a theory or hypothesis or paradigm that explains the phenomena in as elegant a way as possible.

For years missionaries, administrators, and then anthropologists accumulated reports on witchcraft. E. E. Evans-Pritchard, when he was a young man working in the Sudan, had already hit upon the idea that if one sits among a people and listens attentively, one can pick out from their conversation a word or phrase that indicates what they consider their central interest. Among the Azande who lived by the Sudan-Congo border and not far from Uganda, this basic concept was witchcraft. In 1937 Evans-Pritchard published his classic *Witchcraft Among the Azande,* which with Kluckhon's *Navaho Witchcraft* (1944) has been a fundamental work. Despite heavy criticism (the best includes the later thought of Evans-Pritchard himself) its findings and materials can be used in a general way as a guide to our study at this point.

Evans-Pritchard distinguishes between witchcraft and sorcery. Witchcraft proper is a power given to some people that they exercise by psychic means. Sorcery is carried out by conscious intent and involves the use of charms, spells, conscious learning, and experiment. The subject should accordingly be divided up into witchcraft and the tests (oracles), confessions, and purifications that attend it; sorcery, charms, and spells are a parallel topic. All of this must then be located in a general context, which is health, well-being, and fullness of life. This in turn leads to a discussion of the place of "the doctor," "the prophet," and the giver and bringer of blessing.

African Students' Views on Witchcraft

There is so little written by Africans themselves on the subject of witchcraft that I give particular attention to the classroom discussions held by African students in the departments of religious studies at Legon in Ghana, Ibadan and Nsukka in Nigeria, and Makerere in Uganda. The following is a summary of some of the findings. The technical terms were in Twi, Yoruba, Ibo, Luganda, and Swahili, but I here give only the Twi, since it can be related to the Akan "psychology" given earlier.

The prevalence and virulence of witchcraft can be directly related to the health or illness of the community or group one is studying. Evans-Pritchard does not point out how much the Azande suffered since the white man came. Once conquerors and rulers, they were bandied about from Belgians to British; their leaders were shot and the people forcibly resettled along roads. The prominence of witchcraft was related to the white man's incursion; Europeans may not be witches as such, but their coming allowed witchcraft to grow. In some societies a person can be attacked only by a witch who is a blood relative. That is why Europeans in Africa are free of it: Their relatives are far away.

Who, then, are witches? At night the spirit, the personality-soul (*sunsum*), leaves the bodies of some people. This disembodied spirit is the witch (*ɔbayifo*), who is very often a woman, perhaps because women have to suffer more than men. A man can also be a witch, though often there is a special word for a male (*ɔbonsam*). It is like *witch* and *warlock* and *wizard* in English. Females go to the coven (*ɔbayifo fekuw*), and sometimes one sees them flying by, upside down and naked. The hovering, moving lights among the trees and along the shore are the witch lights that come from the witches' mouths and anuses.

The Coven   At the coven, which usually takes place in a tall tree like a silk-cotton, the witches have a leader, a spokesman, and full procedure. It is proposed that so-and-so bring the leg, the lungs, the womb, the penis, and the wealth of such-and-such for them to consume. So-and-so demurs, suggests that it is somebody else's turn. The others submit and do as suggested. They do not literally consume the leg or lungs; they imbibe its substance like Christians in Communion. The next day the victim appears much the same as before, but the parts of the body whose spirit or essence has been eaten waste away.

If one works hard, wastes no money, and still does not become rich, the cause may be witchcraft. The witches cause one's purse to leak, or fingers to fail to grip; they can involve a person in a sudden, crippling accident or law-suit, or they can make someone fail an examination. Some decent person struggling ineffectually with alcohol will say that the witches wish him back to the bottle. The witches will cause someone's cocoa tree to get swollen shoot.

Witches have familiar birds, insects, and animals; that is, spirits embodied in these creatures have entered into a special occult relationship with the witches. Witches send the animals on errands or indeed can themselves change into these animals. The owl, the leopard, the hyena, the crocodile, the snake, and the tsetse fly especially figure as wereanimals.

Helping and Redeeming the Witch   It was generally agreed that some good principle, however vestigial, always worked in witches. With some part of their beings they longed to cease their evil activities. Accordingly, if there were facilities to cleanse them, give them strength to make a new beginning, and protect them from the vindictive, they would confess and be healed. In the meantime one could protect oneself and one's children by the use of amulets and charms (*asuman.*)

In many parts of Africa witchcraft-cleansing cults grew up. Visiting cleansers would call on the chief and offer—for payment—to cleanse the village. Everybody would file by, and some would be accused; they would confess and be cleansed. The colonial authorities put these activities down ruthlessly in many cases because of the opportunities they gave for blackmail and extortion, as well as the horrible nature of some of the ordeals involved. A poison would be prepared. Sometimes it was fed to a chicken, and if the chicken threw up, the person was innocent; if it died, he or she was guilty. At times the poison was used directly on people, and the person who did not vomit the poison died a horrible death. Later his or her body was disposed of with disgrace and ignominy.

The cleansing shrines I visited in Ghana dealt with health as a whole, directing obviously physically ill people to herbalists and hospitals. If someone confessed to witchcraft, the healers cleansed them and made sure society received them back. The fees seemed at least as reasonable as those of the American Medical Association. The government or public suppression of all such anti-witchcraft agencies leaves people unprotected. As so many remark, "The malevolent forces continue and a few pills and potions are not enough." Both Christianity and Islam in Africa are able to be of great assistance to the sufferers. The role of the religious healer and prophet, of the holy man using the Holy Book and lore brought from Arabia and West Asia, fits easily into the witchcraft-healing picture.

Charms and Amulets

From mysterious forces and evil in general, human beings protect themselves worldwide by charms, medallions, and mascots. My mother sending me a Bible to wear over my heart as I went to war in Burma, the guide to the royal Chinese tombs with his little red book—these things are deeply rooted in the human psyche. Similarly, in Africa one sees many people wearing charms. Charms are batteries for the storage of power (*tumi*) that comes from the spirit of the materials from which the charms are made. Thus, charms may consist of sticks from certain powerful trees and roots entwined with fibers, incantations, and sacrifice to ward off other powers. A portion of a broom that has swept toilets, together with a piece of a napkin used in menstruation, enclosed in a charm, is powerful in driving away most spirits good or bad. The *asuman* (charms) may also get some of their strength from the *mmoatia*, "the little folk" of the forest who impart secrets to herbalists, hunters, and prophets seeking visions in the forest. Charms containing verses of the Qur'an get their power from Allah and are very powerful.

Both Africans and Europeans refer to charms as *fetish*. Insofar as the word comes from a Portuguese word meaning "thing made," in this restricted use it is permissible. Given proper ritual and invocation, charms can for certain lengths of time become the locus or dwelling place of spirit-beings and powers, but they are never worshipped in themselves. Uncorrupt African religion does not countenance idolatry.

We have now set before the reader six African systems and indicated the basic pattern or paradigm of the African traditional religion as it emerges from our investigation. We may now go on to study the coming and interaction of the other two main religions of Africa, African Christianity and Islam.

CHAPTER 6

Enter Jesus and Muhammad

Christianity and Islam have been in Africa a long time. Africa has left a deep mark upon both and will affect them even more in the coming century. Since Christianity came first, let us begin by tracing its history in Africa up to the last century.

CHRISTIAN EGYPT

A Ugandan will remind you that Jesus drank Ugandan water, since water from Uganda went down the Nile to Egypt, and Jesus' mother, the Blessed Virgin, drank it and gave him milk. Egypt was one of the first three country-wide conversions that Christianity made. Egyptian Christianity suddenly emerges in Christian history in the second part of the second century, full of energy and power. It produced a succession of great teachers—Origen (about 185–254), Athanasius (about 296–373), Cyril (died 444).

Students in Ghana have for years been studying the life and work of these writers in the original Greek that many Egyptians used during the first centuries. (Later the Egyptian Church used Coptic more and more. Coptic was related to the languages of ancient Egypt, and in many ways Egyptian Christianity continued many features of that earlier civilization.) African students specializing in Christian history greatly admire Origen. He was born of poor parents in lower Egypt. There are a number of indications that he was from the old native substratum, though he thoroughly mastered the know-how of the settlers. He was soon acclaimed a brilliant teacher of Plato's philosophy. Because many young ladies came to his classes and he feared enemies might spread scandalous rumors, he had himself castrated. Afterwards he apologized for this action, because the Church has always opposed such mutilations.

Origen eventually visited and gained acclaim at Rome and other foreign places. He aroused the jealousy of the higher-ups and moved to Caesarea in Palestine. He traveled widely, learning Hebrew and much about Jewish history and scholarship, and he tried to learn all he could about the Gnostics and held discussions with them. He even discovered some ancient scrolls in jars near Jericho. He taught that the love of God was so great, especially as shown in the outstretched arms of Jesus on the cross, that the whole cosmos including the Devil would be reconciled to God in love and joy. He thought of Christian woman and man in their love for one another, which stemmed from God's love, as being the instruments that, through Christ and his body the Church, God would use for this task of cosmic love.

In the meantime, in Egypt the patriarchs of Alexandria were organizing the Egyptian Church, and over a period of two centuries—partly by uncle/nephew succession of immensely able ecclesiastical politicians, partly by sheer numbers and discipline—they brought the Egyptian Church to world leadership. At the Ecumenical Council of 431 at Ephesus, the pope of Alexandria (in the early Church the title was not exclusive to Rome), with the help of the Asian bishops, imposed his will on the Church; the ill-organized Western Church, led by delegates from Rome, obeyed. The Church agreed on the status of the Blessed Virgin; she was called "Mother of God." The Greek is *Theotokos*, which can be translated "she who bore the 'person' who was God." Of course, within this one "person" (a technical term) of Jesus Christ, the Word of God, dwelling in human form, there is complete humanity and a complete divinity. The title Mother of God is one of the titles of Isis, the old African mother goddess. Her blue robe and some other attributes have also passed into Christian tradition concerning the Blessed Virgin.

Let us make no mistake about the Egyptian Church. Its leaders were unsurpassed theologians and metaphysicians. They did not merely borrow from Africa or believe that the Christian teaching was merely the same as the old African teaching. They realized that God has always made himself known and that Christians must be bold enough to recognize and take up this preparation in the older religions for the Gospel. The Egyptian Church loved the teaching about the Logos, the Word of the unutterable God expressed in Jesus the Messiah. In later years the Egyptian Church's opponents organized themselves and gained the help of the imperial soldiery. The Egyptian Church was accused of overemphasizing the divinity of Christ and ignoring the humanity. They were dubbed Monophysites, "the one-nature-of-Christ Christians." The self-styled orthodox Christians at Constantinople and Rome are "two-nature" Christians. It all depends on the meaning of *physis*, which is usually translated "nature." But it can also be legitimately translated "manner of being," hence "person." As it came to be defined in Latin orthodoxy, it was laid down that there is in Jesus Christ one *persona* and two *naturae*, the divine and the human. Though their emphases were different, the various groups of Christians may well have meant basically what the Latins meant, and what the Catholic and Orthodox Churches both mean: Jesus Christ is one, but in that oneness there is complete divinity and complete humanity. The two have been brought together in oneness, harmony, perfection, and permanency. But politicians, ecclesiastical and otherwise, would not let Christian love work out its natural, slow, and painful process. Other considerations—political, social, personal, and economic, and those having to do with "nation," language, class status, and education—took control. The Church, the Body and Bride of Christ, his seamless robe, was rent asunder. The East Roman (Byzantine) government based in Constantinople and its allies found Church dissensions a convenient excuse to help put down Egyptian independence, which was associated with the Egyptian Church.

It is easy to see why Egyptian Christians heartily welcomed the invading Arabs. In one of the miracles of history, a few followers of the prophet Muhammad came into Egypt in C.E. (A.D.) 638, and within two years had driven out the East Romans. The Arabs needed just a little longer to dislodge the imperial Roman power from Alexandria. The Egyptian Church had effectively been taken out of the mainstream of Christian history. During the next centuries, under the tolerant rule of the Muslims, she had a kind of autumnal glow of life and beauty. She contributed greatly to the transmission of Greek and Egyptian wisdom and science to the Arabs and the Islamic World. Coptic physicians and administrators gained world renown. Coptic art, preserved especially in plastic art and textiles, remains one of the great flowerings of Christian art. Eventually, as Egypt was Islamized and rampaging mobs and some caliphs initiated persecution, the Christians became a minority that has survived to this day. Some would say that this minority is more Christian than Europe and America, and more natively Egyptian than the nationalists.

But in the meantime Egyptian Christianity had bequeathed much else to the world Church. She sent missionaries to Ethiopia, which has remained her ecclesiastical daughter to our own day. She also assisted with the Christianization of Nubia, which maintained a black Christianity for centuries. The Christian Church in Egypt has provided some of the best readings of the text of the Bible. Codex Alexandrinus, Codex Vaticanus, and the earliest papyri came from this Church, which also developed some of the basic ideas of the monastic society as we know it in the West. The group of monks was the unit used by Christianity in later centuries to spread its message, carrying the Gospel and civilization across northern Europe and across Russia and Asia to the Pacific. When it came to working among utter barbarians in areas with heavy soils covered with trees and bogs—in England, Ireland, Scandinavia, or eastern Europe—nothing could beat communes of obedient celibates providing free labor, unquenchable enthusiasm, and asking nothing but discipline and suffering. Slave labor and mechanization have both been tried elsewhere and afterward, but both have ghastly side-effects.

The contribution of Egyptian Christianity to a kind of counterculture is hard to assess, though some of our best gnostic and extracanonical manuscripts and teachings go back to this Church. In Egypt there seems to have been much talk of rigid control and absolute orthodoxy, which simple Westerners took seriously and imposed on themselves. Inside the group in Egypt there was tremendous intellectual and spiritual activity, as well as difference of opinion and lively experimentation.

BLACK CHRISTIANITY IN NUBIA AND ETHIOPIA

It is hard to describe the glories of the earliest black Christianity in Nubia and Ethiopia in a few pages. The Nubian Kingdoms occupied the country along the Nile above Egypt, up to the joining of the Blue and White Niles as they come from Ethiopia and Uganda. This country is nowadays part of the Republic of the Sudan. The capital, Khartoum, lies not far from the confluence. The Ethiopian eunuch, "an officer of Queen Candace," whose conversion to Christianity is described in the Book of Acts, Chapter 8, may have come from Meroë, the older African kingdom that formerly lay just south of Egypt.

Individual Christians must have reached Nubia quite soon after the conversion of Egypt in the fourth and fifth centuries. In the sixth century the East Roman empress Theodora sent a Monophysite mission to Nubia, and her husband, Justinian, dispatched an Orthodox mission. Nubian Christianity was born divided. Over the years she approximated more and more the Monophysite Church in Egypt. (Isolated in the far south of India, the St. Thomas Christians did similarly. In central Asia the isolated Christians in Mongolia, Turkestan, and China in the Middle Ages became Nestorians; they allegedly overemphasized the two natures because their contacts were with the Nestorian Churches of Iran and Iraq. Proximity rather than theology decided the rules, especially when a church's home base was hemmed in by Islam.)

Christian Nubia

In Nubia the royal families were converted, and under royal patronage a glorious Christianity emerged. Archaeologists rescued many things in Nubia before the high dam on the Nile flooded the main old areas of habitation and cultivation along the river above Aswan. The cathedral at Faras was found to be a lovely building, with some surviving eighth- to twelfth-century murals that indicate the high level of Nubian Christianity. The Virgin Mary presides over a nativity scene where African cattle and donkeys stand around the baby; three dashing black kings ride up bearing gifts, and two very Fulani-looking nomadic herdsmen-shepherds come up. A black royal lady stands holding what looks like a diaper or wiping cloth. On another wall the black Queen Mother, Martha, is touched by the loving, commissioning, and identifying hand of the Virgin, who is herself the Queen Mother of the heavenly court and presides in her womanly power. Indeed, if we look with African eyes at the infancy narratives of the New Testament, with their detailed genealogies with certain crucial links made through the woman's line, we would learn something about the meaning of the Virgin Birth.

Like redwood trees, Christians need numbers, proximity, and a favorable ecology to survive. Along the Nile south of Egypt, they were far from other Christians. Egyptian Christianity had been overtaken by Muslim rulers. Ethiopia withdrew behind its mountains and marshes. Muslim adventurers and traders pursuing gold and slaves penetrated more and more, and nomads from the desert found the Christian cultivators easy prey, dependent as they were on the river for irrigation, strung out along the thin ribbons of shore-line. As the centuries wore on, Christianity began to fade. When the sultans of Egypt in the twelfth and thirteenth centuries began to interfere, and members of the royal families allied themselves with the sultans and Islam to gain advantages, the end was in sight.

Christian Ethiopia

In Ethiopia, legend has it that in the days of King Solomon the Queen of Sheba was converted, and when Christianity came along Ethiopia became Christian. If so, we may suppose that the Ethiopian Jews, the Falasha, were those who did not convert. Perhaps, like the Bayudaya in Uganda in modern times, they were Africans who had access to the Jewish Bible (known to Christians as the Old Testament) and modeled their religion on it. The New Testament and early Christian sources indicate very early connections between Christianity and Ethiopia, but much geographical confusion clouds the issues.

With the fourth century we stand on firmer historical ground. Two boys from Syria were stranded in Ethiopia and grew up there. They returned from a visit home commissioned by the archbishop of Alexandria in Egypt to lead the Ethiopian Church. The Church flourished and kept up the strong link with Alexandria. Until recent times, the head of the Church, the Abuna, had to be sent from Egypt. In every other respect the Ethiopian Church was highly localized. Its architecture, its singing, and its services were very African, and the emperor had a very special place in it. The clergy were mainly ordinary people living as farmers on church land and conducting services. The monasteries preserved the old Egyptian-style individual hermitages clustered around the common buildings. Rowing out across a mountain lake or going through forests and over torrents and boulders to an Ethiopian monastery remains an unforgettable experience.

When the Muslims took Egypt, eliminated Christianity from southern Arabia, and eventually cut off Ethiopia from the sea, this black Church turned in on itself—to quote Gibbon's resounding phrase, "the world forgetting, by the world forgot." The medieval history of the Ethiopian Church is of great interest, but we can only hint at the Church's many achievements. It continued to convert non-Christian, non-Muslim tribes, and it continued to relate Christianity to the problems of daily life. In all powerful empires with monarchs who beget many children, civil war breaks out as soon as the emperor dies; then the claimant must succeed as emperor, submit to death at once, or die fighting. The histories of the Ottoman Turkish and the Mughal Indian empires are only two examples. Medieval Ethiopia invented Mount Gishen. It was a plateau with full facilities for a comfortable life, but no unguarded entrances and exits. All but the chosen successor were sent up there, and a trusty family of gatekeepers saw to it for centuries that none came out except with official permission.

At a time when much of the world was in what are called the Dark Ages, Ethiopia produced a Christian architecture of its own. It ranged from the churches at Lalibela, which were carved out of one solid rock like the world-famous Kailasha Temple of Shiva in central India, to little village churches. At the center of all of these is a consecrated slab, the *tabot*, on which the Eucharist is offered. Only priests in ritual purity may enter the innermost circular sanctuary. Around it in widening circles, like the African concentric thatched-roof buildings sheltering them, come other officiants: the singers, communicants, auditors, and finally penitents and "hearers." At great festivals the *tabot* is carried in procession on a man's head, and sheltered like a king by an umbrella. Drummers, dancers, and singers join in. *Timkat*, a festival in which people pass through a river along with their cattle and holy objects and then make "tabernacles" (camp out), is an especially joyful time and gives the young people an opportunity to get to know one another.

The art and literature of the medieval Ethiopian Church has also lived on. A St. George on a stallion, much in the style of early eastern Christianity, rides down a very African crocodile; a blue-robed Blessed Virgin and child with Ethiopian features give a blessing, the Blessed Mother holding a cloth in the African fashion to mop up rather than to diaper. Beautifully illustrated manuscripts preserve versions of early Christian works that were little known until recently in the West. Local writers excelled in hagiology, the composition of stories about saints, their adventures, and the wonders they performed. It is a wonderful and beautiful world that has as much to teach outsiders as Tibet has. May it be as successful in doing so! We now turn thousands of miles westward and go back to the second century C.E. (A.D.).

CHRISTIANITY IN ROMAN AFRICA

Far to the west, across the African continent from Egypt and Ethiopia, was the second great region to become Christian. (The third was Asia Minor. No European country followed suit for a century or two.) This was the original "Africa," Africa Proconsularis of the Romans, Ifrikiyya of the Arabs, with Roman Numidia and Mauretania, the Arab Far West, the Maghrib. Today these areas are known in rough approximation as Tunisia, Algeria, and Morocco, and the great stretches of the mighty Sahara to their south.

The African Proto-Martyrs and a Magisterial Teacher of Western Christianity

About A.D. 180, the Church of Roman Africa suddenly steps onto the stage of history. The first voices heard are of very ordinary women and men declaring their enthusiasm for Jesus and their refusal to give in to police bullying and imperial punishment. Soon we hear the reverberating tones of an authoritative teacher and orator. Tertullian of Carthage (about A.D. 160–225) had mastered the language and thought of the imperialist Romans; using Latin, he hammered out formulae and phrases that have dominated the Western Church ever since. The Western doctrine of the Trinity (three persons in one substance) and the doctrine of Christology (two natures, divine and human, in one person) owe their precision of formulation to him.

In Tertullian one also finds traces of other doctrines much beloved by various sections of the Western Church. For example, there is in his writings a doctrine of atonement (at-one-ment) firmly based on the idea of substitutionary sacrifice. Tertullian also probably owed something to the native African teaching that is found, for instance, among the Berber tribes that have been in northwest Africa since the beginning of history and are still there. He may have owed something also to the old Carthaginians who settled in Africa as early as the eighth century B.C.E. (B.C.) and brought with them from Phoenicia doctrines similar to those mentioned in the Jewish Bible, the Christian Old Testament. Some of the most influential early translations of the Bible into Latin were made in Roman Africa and helped to shape the thinking of the Latin Fathers from Tertullian to Augustine, and hence to influence the whole of Western Christianity.

Cyprian of Roman Africa, Doctor of the Western Church

Tertullian was followed by Cyprian of Carthage, who died C.E. (A.D.) 258 as a martyr by the sword of the imperial executioner. Cyprian taught much about the Church as a body, as a community. Every member had a place and could depend on the body for support and sustenance. A person could die assured of decent burial and the proper assistance to spouse and young. The other side of this teaching was the rigorous exclusion of those outside the family or those who by deviant thinking and recalcitrance put themselves outside the group. At all times the community was willing to welcome sincere inquirers of all races and classes, and to receive back those of its own who unconditionally repented.

Augustine of Hippo, Father of Western Thought

In due time African Christianity produced Augustine of Hippo Regius ([A.D.] C.E. 354–430; his birthplace is in what is now Algeria). This man's thought dominated Europe for a thousand years, and remains fundamental to this day. He had for some years been a follower of the teachings of the Iranian gnostic Mani, who was suspicious of the body and its desires; but though Augustine may have retained some of this thinking, he rejected Mani. His basic background was African Christianity; he had no class or economic or academic group to give him eminence, and his town was very far from any center of vital public opinion. He knew no Hebrew and very little Greek, and he may not even have learned a word of Germanic origin from the fair-skinned, blue-eyed Vandals who invaded his country toward the end of his life. He had a powerful mother whose name, Monica, honored an old African goddess; he knew the general teaching of the African Church and had a superb command of Latin, the lingua franca of the Western world, as his major assets.

The Decline of Roman African Christianity

Christianity in Roman Africa was grievously divided before Saint Augustine's day between those who gave their allegiance to catholic, ecumenical, worldwide Christianity and those who believed that their own local form held the truth and that the others had left it. Then the Vandals destroyed the economic basis of Roman Africa. The East Romans carried out a reconquest that reduced Roman Africa to impotence. When the Muslims came in the middle of the seventh century they met with stiff resistance; then suddenly, early in the eighth century, the Berbers left Christianity and became the mainspring in the Muslim invasions that overran Spain and half of France. Muslim seafarers based in Africa even managed to raid the shrine of St. Peter in Rome.

After the first love affair between Christianity and Africa, which ended with the coming of Islam, in most places Christianity had to wait until the fifteenth century—some eight hundred years—before trying

again. Let us consider the courtship of the other suitor who had mean-
while appeared on the scene.

THE FIRST ISLAMIC CENTURIES

Islam in Northern Africa

At first the Arabs were content with quickly overrunning the old areas
of Roman imperialism in Egypt and North Africa. In North Africa, before long the bulk of the population went over to Islam, and within a
few centuries the great new Islamic encampments like Kairouan began
to produce scholars of more than local eminence. In due time cities like
Fez also came into prominence; and in the west, the Maghrib, together
with its daughter Spain, produced some of the world's finest poetry,
philosophy, and architecture. Abd al-Rahman ibn Khaldun of Tunis
(1332–1406) was a thinker who ranks high in the Muslim world, though
not as high as Augustine does in the Western world. His *Introduction to
World History* perhaps stands beside *The City of God* in brilliance, and
surpasses it in research and logic. A near contemporary of his, Muhammad ibn Battuta of Tangier, was the greatest traveller before the discovery of the New World. He surpasses Marco Polo in the number of places
visited and many others in the depth of insight of the comments he
makes on the people and things he sees. We shall meet him again later.

In Egypt, Islam spread from the new city that was to be called Cairo
and from the top downward. By the fourteenth century Egypt had become a venerable storehouse of resources and learning for Islam, still
standing serene and powerful when Baghdad, Samara, and Samarkand
had been destroyed by the Mongols.

Islam into Black Africa

When the Arabs reached the south of Egypt they were repelled by the
"eye-smiting" Nubians and made a pact with them. At first they made
little progress across the Sahara. By sea, however, Islam was in immediate touch with Africa. Arab sailors thought nothing of the voyage from
Jeddah to what we now call the Sudan. In the lifetime of the Prophet
his relatives and friends crossed to Africa and made their way to the
Ethiopian court, where they were well received. Indeed, the negus (the
emperor of Ethiopia) is one of the rulers Muslim tradition says was
invited to embrace Islam by the Prophet himself. Muslims could very
early ride the ships of southwestern Arabia as they voyaged on the
monsoon winds down the East African coast to the mouth of the Zambesi and beyond. Despite the spectacular length of this line of communication down eastern Africa, communication did not reach inland until
the nineteenth century. The most notable achievements were across the
Sahara in West Africa.

Islam across the Great Desert

We do not know why the Romans, the Christians of Roman Africa, and the first Muslims of the Maghrib did not effectively penetrate the Sahara to black Africa. For people like the Arabs, used to desert and camels, the Sahara must have seemed positively homey. Presumably, since religious enthusiasm was never lacking, when they had digested their conquests in North Africa, some propagators of Islam were attracted across the Sahara primarily by economic reasons. Perhaps the trade in gold and in slaves triggered the movement. Perhaps the causes were ecological and logistical. When transportation of goods became feasible by the development of routes based on the availability of drinking water, traffic increased. The first Muslim missionary is not usually a man of war; he is a wandering scholar-trader-holy man. He travels from place to place teaching about God and living on trading and the charity of the local people. He is a man powerful in prayer who can accept a reward for his efforts in producing fertility in people, fields, and animals. Perhaps he has powers of healing; his prayers can bring good luck and ward off evil. He may be given a local wife and found a family that will travel, spreading Islamic holiness. Then, too, Muslim traders and merchants come and start a business. Such men will marry local wives out of the need for love and fellowship, and then set them up as the managers of the local branches, for they need a reliable local person to look after business. The serenity, good cheer, and high civilization of these Muslims soon attract local folk, so the faith spreads of its own accord, as Jesus says in the Gospel. (Muslims accept Jesus as a foremost prophet and authoritative teacher, except where they consider that Christians have twisted the Gospel to their own meanings.)

Muslims Ever Self-Reforming

By the eleventh century Islam had spread sufficiently in the western Sahara for there to be a need for reformation. It is usual for Muslims to accept into their faith anyone who declares belief in Allah and his Prophet. He or she will be taught the elements of belief and practice, given a ritual bath, and left to follow in the straight path of Islam. (Circumcision is customary for men, but many African peoples practice it anyway.) As Islam is lived out in daily life, there are always those who will become aware of the highest standards as practiced by the elite. Perhaps a teacher will come and tell people of these standards; perhaps the people will observe them in the books that become available; perhaps they will observe them as they travel, especially on the Ḥajj, the great pilgrimage to Mecca. A reformer arises and gathers followers who carefully practice every detail of Islam as they know it. They realize that those around them are falling far short of the ideal. They try to bring about a reform. Sometimes this is done by peaceful permeation.

From the twelfth century onward, the mystical Sufi brotherhoods began to influence Africa. Over the years they have adapted to circumstances. For example, they organized the growing of cash crops and supported political parties, but they have always helped simple folk reach the loving, living heart of Islam. The Qadiriyya, with its orthodox keeping of the law and its charity, and the Tijaniyya, with their love of dreams and visions and their looking to the Resurrection, have been the most important of the brotherhoods. But even earlier than the brotherhoods, from the eleventh century on, there were reformers who took to arms and holy war (*jihad*) as a means of reformation and of spreading the faith among non-Muslims.

The interplay of these elements—the coming of holy men and traders and warriors, the conversion of some local people, the wider acceptance of at least some elements of Islam on a larger scale, the rise and work of reformers, consolidation, the further spread of some thoroughgoing Islam with general Islamic influence over larger groups—has been a constantly recurring pattern. Scholars see the pattern as the coming of Islam, its quarantine or encapsulation (the time when it is contained by the traditional religions and exists apart from them), a time of mixing, then reformation and conversion. Probably it is best not to see any pattern as exclusive, bearing in mind that Africans in those days not only thought and acted as individuals but also as members of a group or tribal body; they did not believe that tradition and Islam excluded each other.

In the following historical outline, we can see these patterns and processes at work during the next centuries. We must also mention the great empires and civilizations that arose, because they are justly part of worldwide black pride.

The Rise of the Great Black Empires

In the eleventh century in the far west of Africa, Abdullah ibn Yasin (d. 1059), whose mother was a Berber, was so distressed by the lukewarm Islam of his people that he withdrew to a *ribat* (retreat, "monastery") near the Atlantic. From here issued forth men of the *ribat*—*murabitun*, "Almoravids"—who carried reform through the Sahara and North Africa up to Spain. In the meantime, in the old black African kingdom of Ghana, a Muslim city had existed side by side with a city of the traditionalists. In some places kings and other leaders had converted to Islam when they saw prayers for rain or fertility answered. In 1076, when Ghana disintegrated, many Muslims were scattered abroad. They came to be affected by the purer reformed Islam preached by the Almoravids and carried it toward the forest belt in the south. Some settled in places like Timbuktu (founded around 1100) and Jenne (founded about 1250). These two cities became great centers of the finest Muslim learning, in constant touch with Mecca, Cairo, Fez, and Tunis. Timbuktu has been a university town at least as long as has Oxford.

A Muslim World Traveller in Medieval Africa

Islam continued its steady spread in Africa. From the fourteenth century we are lucky enough to have the firsthand account of Ibn Battuta, a Muslim traveller (born in Tangier in 1304) who visited black Africa right down the eastern coast to Kilwa in southern Tanzania, as well as West Africa to the heart of the old black kingdom of Mali, which lay not far from the upper waters of the Niger. In East Africa he found a flourishing Islam in some of the Arab towns of what we would call Somalia, Kenya, and Tanzania, but little contact with the hinterland except for some trading and slave raiding. In Mali he found the royal family and the officials deeply devoted to many features of Islam. The fast was being kept, the Qur'an learned. Some people, notably Mansa Musa, had gone on the pilgrimage. But in the nonsegregation and nakedness of women, the old gentleman found much to disturb him.

In due time political leadership passed from Mali further eastward to the kingdom of Songhai, in the great bend of the Niger. Here again Islam was able to spread and to influence especially the ruling and the mercantile classes. In the 1590s the sultan of Morocco sent an army consisting mainly of Spanish renegades from Christianity and foreign slave soldiers to gain better access to the gold mines. The army conquered Songhai and then presided over the ruins for a while. By this time the Portuguese had reached the West African coast as well as the mouth of the Congo, and had circumnavigated Africa. A new era in the history of African religion had opened. Before we come to that, let us glance briefly west to east across Africa.

ISLAM IN AFRICA FROM THE FIFTEENTH
TO THE NINETEENTH CENTURIES

Islam penetrated across the desert and grasslands to a line that ran roughly at 10° north—that is, about halfway between the equator and the Tropic of Cancer. In the far west it had a secure foothold in the plateau and highland of the Futa, from where one day it could spread into Senegal, Sierra Leone, and Liberia, as well as eastward. In the heyday of the empire of Mali, Islam had made great strides. Yet large masses of people in the fields and villages, in the cliffs and along the river, remained unaffected by Islam. Indeed, peoples following traditional cults, such as the Bambara and Mossi, proved highly resistant at this time. Farther south of Mali and Ghana, in the kingdoms of Asante and Dahomey, as well as in the forests of the Ivory Coast, Muslims were welcomed as holy men of power, as traders and scribes, but were effectively sealed off as far as any major spread of their religion was concerned. Going eastward along the Niger from Songhai and Mali and coming to what we today call northern Nigeria and the area of Lake Chad, and the cities and kingdoms of Hausa-land and of Kanem-Bornu, we find that Islam was brought in by merchants and holy men from the Mali and Songhai areas as well as directly across the Sahara by Taureg and other travelling scholars and holy men. Contact across the desert by caravan with Tunisia, Libya, and Egypt was regular and comparatively easy. Good progress was being made, but the people did not hurry into Islam. They admitted Muslims as individuals and in small groups; then the rulers adopted some elements of Islam, and many began to profess Islam while retaining much of the old. Still, great pockets of the country remained unpenetrated by the faith. The whole of the south, including the land of the Yoruba, was hardly touched, though no doubt some Muslim merchants, travellers, and slaves passed through those lands to the sea. It was not until late in the eighteenth century that a full, true reformation and propagation were to take place. The bringing of Islam to the Yoruba really started in the nineteenth century.

Going farther east from Lake Chad, we learn from Ibn Battuta that some of the kings of Nubia had left Christianity for Islam. Archaeology shows us that Christianity survived with some vigor until the late thirteenth century. In the eastern horn of Africa, Islam had gained a deep hold among the people of the coastlands in what we today call Eritrea, or northeast Ethiopia and Somalia. From here an onslaught on the kingdom of Ethiopia could begin. Along the east coast the line of Muslim penetration swings south from 10° north and goes along the coast (Arabic *sawahil*, hence "Swahili") as far south as the mouth of the Zambesi.

The geographical situation is comparatively easy to describe; it is harder to reconstruct the day-to-day position of Islam in tropical Africa in the premodern period. However, the writings of some observers using Arabic, and the earliest works in African languages that began to be written in Arabic script—for instance, Hausa and Swahili—give us valuable insights. First of all, indigenous situations in which the basics of Islam could be communicated had been created. This meant not only the hammering out of a vocabulary in the local languages but in daily life and thought. We may briefly consider these under the headings of the standard five duties of Islam. First, there is the declaration and belief that Allah is One and Muhammad is his Prophet. To be strict and logical, this statement could exclude most of the African world of spirit and divinity. Uncompromising African Muslim reformers understood it so. (It equally excludes any kind of divinity in Jesus Christ and any notion of the Trinity.) But through the centuries many sincere Africans, while believing in Allah as the one true God, have identified him with one of their Supreme Beings and conceded a lesser divine potency to the spirit powers of the ancestors and ancestresses, and to the various subsupreme manifestations of divinity in which their traditionalist brothers and sisters believe. The strict followers of the Muslim divine law were sometimes prepared to wait a while and then carry on an all-out campaign to purge the ultimate sin of association, associating any with Allah.

The next great obligation is to perform the set prayers five times a day, and if possible to attend at least the noon prayer on Friday (the Day of Congregation) at the mosque. To judge by the Swahili and Hausa cases, black Africans have joined in heartily here and in the keeping of the two great festivals. The nonobligatory prayers, including prayer for rain, for fertility, or just for communion with Allah, have been powerful points of attraction to non-Muslims.

The Ḥajj is the great pilgrimage to Mecca. Thousands of black pilgrims make the journey, if they can do so, once in a lifetime. The hardships of the way, walking across Africa, sailing along the coasts in crazy boats, loaded like cattle into vehicles or aircraft, are all forgotten in the joy of being on the pilgrimage and bringing back news of how things Islamic are really practiced. Perhaps the diseases contracted and survived on the pilgrimage meant Africa did not lose nine-tenths of its people to new diseases on first meeting Europeans, as happened in Oceania and the Americas.

Islam asks for a tithing of income, and with the money gathered provides facilities not only for worship but for welfare for the disadvantaged. The way in which Muslims looked after their poor, buried the dead with dignity, and provided for widows and orphans obviously created a deep impression on Africans.

The rigors of the lunar month of fasting, Ramaḍān, are a terror to converts in Europe and America, but many Africans seem to appreciate the benefits of the fast. In any case, in old Africa hunger was well known when the stored crop ran out and the new crop had not yet been harvested.

The full imposition of Islamic law meant an interdict on alcohol, drugs, certain forms of graphic art, and music. None of these comes easily to new Muslims. Similarly, Islam's attitude toward the body, sexuality, and women differs a good deal from many of the traditional African points of view. Islam requires that the body be covered, that women be given their own proper place and rights, and that they not mingle with men other than husbands or relatives except in carefully guarded circumstances. Some Africans found no difficulty in practicing both Islamic and traditional ways of life, but at regular intervals reformers would demand the keeping of the divine law.

The allegation that Islam is an easy religion that Africans, Indians, or Indonesians took on only in outward appearance is a falsification created by nineteenth-century Europeans who had not tried to practice Islam themselves. But if someone tries to fulfill any part of the divine law, great help is given both by the rest of the community and by the divine. The Sufi brotherhoods did a great deal to spread Islam and assist the newly won. Their sense of community, their mutual help and cooperation, their fellowship with one another, with world Islam, and with the divine in mysticism—quite apart from the political and economic power they came to wield—were a notable source of strength.

In many parts of Africa, the little mosque schools run by the local prayer leader and his wife provided the elements of writing, arithmetic, and knowledge of a wider world centuries before universal primary education became established in Europe. To this day, it fills the mind of the sympathetic visitor with wonder to see the age-old syllabus and discipline; many Muslims look back with affection to their teacher and the habits of study and self-discipline they learned.

From the areas it had already entered by the thirteenth and fourteenth centuries, Islam had secure bases from which to penetrate the great western rain forests and reach the West African coast. From the eastern coast it could go inland to the great lakes, then down the tributaries of the Congo (Zaïre) to the Atlantic.

Amazingly enough, the natural advance of Islam across Africa ceased for centuries. The Christians flatter themselves that they stopped it, and many Muslims believe them. The real reasons Islam stopped are that something had happened to Islam internally and, above all, that African traditional religions had found a balance with Islam and were holding their own. Similarly, Christianity in Europe, Hinduism in India, and Buddhism in central Asia managed to stop the advance of Islam around the same time until the European imperialists and the modern world for the moment destroyed their equilibrium.

CHRISTIANITY TRIES AGAIN

The Portuguese Voyages and Catholic Missions

By the end of the fifteenth century the Portuguese had sailed around black Africa's west, south, and east coasts. They established trading posts in a number of places. On their ships and at their places of trade were men who were devoted to spreading Christianity. There was no means of travelling other than with the Portuguese. There were always some who questioned the behavior of the imperial power and its representatives, but most humans use rather than question whatever facilities are at hand. It is obvious as one studies this period that the Africans gave a most generous and hospitable welcome to Christianity, but whatever success Christianity might have attained was obliterated by European imperialism, atrocious behavior, and intolerance for other religions or even for Christians other than the European kind. The Portuguese even insisted that the Pope should be approached only through the metropolitan country, Portugal. In addition, they imported the fatal mistake of supposing that Christianity in Africa was a kind of crusade against Islam, thus making enemies of co-workers.

At a time when the words *Portuguese* and *imperialist* stink in every African nostril, the memory of the Portuguese use of Christianity and of Christianity's cooperation with the Portuguese does Christianity in Africa no good. But, while appreciating this as students, we have to see the facts as some of the greatest Africans see them. In a conversation with me in 1960, Peter Dagadu, a notable Ghanaian nationalist and church leader, remarked of the missionaries: "When a porter brings you a package containing valuables, do you enquire about his friends? You give him his due and let him go."

Fifteenth-Century Christianity in Ghana

At Elmina in Ghana stands a magnificent castle restored by the government of Kwame Nkrumah. It was originally built in the 1480s with stone floated out in ballast from Portugal. The chapel is named after St. James, the Killer of Moors (Muslims). Santiago in Chile and many other places in the Latin American world have the same dedication. On the other side of Africa, at Mombasa, frowns Fort Jesus, built in the sixteenth century in the best Renaissance humanistic style. Under the shadow of such forts, Portuguese priests celebrated their holy mysteries and taught a few children, while the soldiers and merchants carried on their more nefarious activities. Not far from the mouths of the Niger, at the kingdom of Benin, the Portuguese came to the king as suppliants asking to trade and to preach their religion. They were given a place some distance from the capital and kept under surveillance. In Benin art we catch glimpses of this visitor with his firearms, potbelly, and avaricious eyes. We also see crosses of beautiful workmanship on the chests of African noblemen and warriors.

Christianity in the Congo Kingdom

A short distance south of the mouth of the Congo (Zaïre), the kings of Congo in the late fifteenth and early sixteenth centuries received the Portuguese most liberally. Members of the royal family and many others became Christian. Indeed, one of the highest members of the black nobility became the first black bishop of the Catholic Church in modern times. But the Africans found it difficult to gain direct access to the Pope because the Portuguese claimed all rights of patronage. Then Portuguese slavers and settlers helped break up the kingdom, and with its death went the most promising Christian Church of the Africa of that day. Much had been achieved, including the first printed texts in an African language. A last glimpse of this church is given in the story of Beatrix Kimpa Vita. She began to be possessed and to speak in behalf of the divine. It was said to be St. Anthony speaking in her. She preached of a black Christ and carried out healing. Gradually, people looking for deliverance from the foreigners gathered around her. She gave birth to a son who had promise of leading his people, and she was burned at the stake in 1706. In modern times, independent and independence-seeking Christians have been superabundantly active in the same part of Africa.

Christianity in Zimbabwe

Inland from the mouth of the Zambesi various African civilizations, including the one that built the great walls explorers called Zimbabwe, had grown up. When the Portuguese came here in the sixteenth and seventeenth centuries, they heard of *Regnum Monomotapae*, the kingdom of the Mwene (Lord) Mutapa. Downriver and by the sea, Portuguese traders managed to establish themselves in the age-old trade in Sofala gold, despite the Muslims who had preceded them. But missionaries penetrated to the kingdom itself and gained conversions in the royal family. The inevitable reaction followed; some glorious martyrdoms were attained. But long-term results were impaired by the policies of the Portuguese colonial power established precariously on the coast, in what would one day grow into the colony of Mozambique.

East African Christianity from the Sixteenth to the Eighteenth Centuries

On the coast of East Africa in the old, established, largely Muslim cities like Kilwa, Mombasa, and Malindi, Christianity may have met with some success, but this success was inevitably obliterated by the effects of Portuguese politics and methods. The Portuguese sacked Kilwa in 1505. Recently, archaeologists found the bones of many people left unburied at a period later than the sacking. These may be the remains of the Christians massacred by the local people when the inevitable response came. The archaeologists, who were from Britain, wanted to leave the bones around in heaps; the local Muslims insisted that they be given a decent burial. At Mombasa, the Christians converted the king, but he came to believe that his conversion was only a part of the total takeover, and he returned to Islam and led the massacre of the Portuguese and of any Christians he could reach.

The Portuguese and Ethiopia

The episode of Christopher da Gama giving his life to save the Ethiopian Church has in it both epic and tragedy. Equally great is the story of his Muslim opponent, Ahmed Gran, "the Left-Handed." In the mid-sixteenth century Ahmed had rallied the Somali and other nomads of the Horn and was systematically overcoming the Ethiopian Empire. A small Portuguese expedition landed; a contemporary manuscript shows its leader, so handsome in his short Portuguese cloak and his youthful strength. Christopher did not wait for his Ethiopian friends. He won engagement after engagement. Then Ahmed took his encampment by surprise and executed him. Some of the Portuguese, notably their experts in weaponry and gunpowder, escaped. With the help of these technicians, the Ethiopians killed "the Left-Handed" and drove out his followers. But then the Portuguese, especially their churchmen, took on too much. The emperor was made a Catholic, and the Ethiopian Church was to be merged with the Roman Catholic Church under Portuguese leadership. Naturally the foreigners were turned out, and with Muslim help Ethiopia gratefully resumed her isolation among her mountains and wilderness.

CHAPTER 7

Things Fall Apart— The Center Holds

THE SLAVE TRADE

The history of Africa from the sixteenth to the mid-nineteenth centuries is overcast by the calamity, atrocity, and tragedy known as the slave trade. Various forms of slavery had existed within traditional Africa. These varied from the enslavement of prisoners of war and criminals convicted of capital crimes, to children who were handed over during famine so they would not starve to death. In nearly every case, the slave had a place in society; often he or she became a member of a clan or family, and in a few generations the slave's offspring found themselves free. Arabs, North Africans, and others who had been Islamized used black Africans as slaves in the same way that they used Europeans or Asians or anyone else who fell outside the *dar al Islam*, the household of Islam.

The spirit of Islam's rules on slavery is that Allah loves the freeing and good treatment of slaves. Within ritual and worship, the slave and the free person are equal in the sight of Allah. No one would deny that slavery in Islam held its unimaginable horrors—the great slave revolts, such as those mounted by the blacks working the salt mines of Iraq, and the position of girls captured in villages of the savannah and marched off across the Sahara to the harems of the Middle East are a reminder. But the Arab historians also tell of how many African slaves could, and often did, find themselves in positions of honor, power, and comfort. Some of their children found themselves inheriting sultanates and even imamates, or at least freedom.

Christianity was born into the world of the Jews and Graeco-Romans.

The Jewish Bible (which the Christians adopted as their Old Testament) stated that slavery was repugnant to God, especially when it occurred among brothers and sisters. God looked to the Jubilee, when freedom for both the people and the land would be granted. The Greeks spoke much of freedom but did little to ensure that slaves, women, and barbarians received its benefits. The Romans allowed torture for slaves, crucifixion for those who revolted, and the systematic use of slaves in plantation and factory. Christianity attempts to bring the human race back to God; social, economic, and political consequences follow, but they come as the corporate being, humanity-in-Christ, works them out. As African Christians love to point out, in Christ there is no slave or free person, Greek or barbarian, male or female—they are a new creation (St. Paul to the Galatians, chapter 3, verses 28 and 29; chapter 6, verse 15). But the humanity element of the equation *Church = humanity-in-Christ* may need centuries and a lot of pushing before the implications are worked out.

Accordingly, by the fifth century slavery of the old kind had died out in western Christendom. Muslim Arabs and Berbers conquered Spain and Portugal, and during the slow centuries of the reoccupation by "Christian" powers, new ideas that were neither truly Islamic nor Christian entered the heads of the people who spearheaded the encounter of European and African, Christianity and Islam. Early in their fifteenth-century voyages along the African coast, the Portuguese kidnapped Africans and took them back to be bought and sold and made to work like cattle. When they and the Spaniards needed labor in the Americas, where the unfortunate natives were dying out especially in the mines and plantations, it was economically logical to import black workers, who had a phenomenal ability to work and survive.

Christianity found itself facing several dilemmas. The Bible clearly teaches that all humans are sisters and brothers. Yet the chosen ones in the human family are meant to tend—that is, look after and develop—the face of the earth. The Church saw itself as the protector of the native Americans, in the face of Spanish soldiers and settlers. Bringing in the blacks might save the others, but slave-raiding and enslavement were against all Christian principle. Eternal salvation was more important than temporary comfort, and both blacks and the peoples of America could be taught and baptized. Equally, God did not approve of anyone's life on earth being made hell. So the arguments drifted to and fro while the economic planners, bankers, politicians, and exploiters went their way and Africans and native Americans suffered in ways that exceed description.

In the seventeenth and eighteenth centuries, British and Dutch and other chartered companies developed the whole situation into the fabric of a world economy and power play. The background of these merchants and their employees was Christian, but they were engaged in commerce, in business. In documents from those days, we may trace the process by which Christian principles were at last applied. For instance, in the diaries and writings of John Newton we see a man who was baptized in infancy and brought up as a Christian being employed on a ship that is ordered to pick up a cargo of slaves. After some time in this work, in which humans alternate with other "cargoes," he is suddenly converted to the living Christ of the Evangelical revival. Now he sees the implications of his religion. He devotes the rest of his life and all of his energy to ending this infamy. Such writings as Newton's also give us some notion of the incredible sufferings of the slaves—especially the women—and of the situation of the European sailors, whose plight and mortality rates indicate some more of the price paid for the accumulation of capital that is said to have been necessary for the industrial revolution to take place. A few slaves literate in European languages and Arabic have also left us accounts, but so far no such work from a female slave's hand has emerged into prominence. At long last in the nineteenth century, Christianity contributed richly to the ending of the trade. By that time, philanthropy as well as changing economic and political factors had an important part to play.

The slave trade across the Sahara and the Indian Ocean and down the Nile intensified to a holocaustic crescendo as the interior regions of the upper Nile, the Congo, and the Great Lakes were "developed" by Swahili and Arab conquistadores and merchants. In places it was not effectively checked until the 1890s. The short period after the Atlantic trade was stopped and before wholesale European government and economic interests took over Africa was a great moment for Christianity to try to establish itself again without any criminal companions.

CHRISTIANITY IN AFRICA AFTER
SLAVERY AND BEFORE COLONIALISM

Recently a new method for spreading Christianity had evolved. The early Church had had local units that sent people out to start other little churches. The medieval Church had had the monastic society, a self-sustaining celibate commune whose members worked and taught at little or no cost to the Mother Church. Now groups of concerned and generous Christians came together to commission and finance a missionary society. It was the counterpart of a chartered company and could be unconnected with governments. Since it collected and recruited from the very rich and very poor alike, it is difficult to stereotype in terms of class structure or economic base. By necessity the people sent in the early days were very close to the Africans they came to serve; by necessity they had to make every use of African potential and resources.

Examples in West and East Africa
During this time there were some notable achievements. As early as 1787 the Church was being established in Sierra Leone among freed

slaves. Over the years a community was built up in which black missionaries to the rest of Africa were recruited and trained, and very valuable experience of the meeting of Christianity with African traditional religion and Islam was gained. In 1822, aboard the first ship bringing black immigrants back from America to Africa, the first church to work in what was to be called Liberia was formed. American blacks have continued to contribute richly to African Christianity in many places besides Liberia, but Christianity in Liberia especially remains a tribute to their achievement. Within the Christian group many people stand out; here we can only mention a select few.

In 1838 Thomas Birch Freeman, whose father was a black, arrived in Gold Coast (Ghana) on behalf of a British Methodist group. He made great use of local teachers, visited the kings of Asante and Dahomey (Benin), and started work among the Yoruba. Samuel Adjai Crowther (1806–91), a Yoruba slave freed by the British Navy and resettled in Sierra Leone, was sent by the Church Missionary Society (Anglican/Episcopal) to Nigeria. He was a favorite with Queen Victoria and became the first African Anglican bishop of modern times. He evangelized large parts of his Yoruba homeland, and his scholarly imprint on Yoruba religious language remains a monument to him. (He was not afraid to borrow words from Islam.) He started missions in the Niger delta and then inland on the Niger.

In Buganda, on Africa's greatest lake, the Church Missionary Society and the Roman Catholic White Fathers' Society arrived within two years of one another. Both depended on the goodwill of the Kabaka Mutesa. He played them against each other and against the Muslims who had come to the Ganda court from Swahili-land some forty years earlier. By the time the Christians arrived, he had carried out a great persecution of Muslims in which hundreds of young Baganda witnessed as martyrs to the way of Allah and Muhammad. A consummate politician, who in his century ranks with Metternich and Bismarck, he used all the newcomers against overweening traditionalists and against one another. After the death of this master politician in 1884, his son, Mwanga, did not wield the powers as well. He persecuted the Christians and put hundreds of Ganda Christians, both Protestant and Catholic, to death. (Truly, both church and mosque in Uganda do not lack martyrs.) A civil war broke out in which the great British colonialist Lord Lugard insisted on adding, as Abu Mayanja, the Muslim Ugandan orator, has put it, "the utterance of the Maxim gun from Mount Rubaga [Kampala] to the maxims of Jesus from the Mount."

David Livingstone and Mary Slessor:
Two Great Scottish Missionaries

David Livingstone, a member of the Scottish landless proletariat who was rendered destitute by the industrial revolution, studied medicine as he worked in a mill. He then went as a missionary to southern Africa. His great safaris on foot from one side of Africa to another and his love and respect for Africans, including his fellow medical practitioners dubbed "witch doctors," were surpassed only by the hospitality and generosity of Africa. In no other continent could a person with no resources of his own have accomplished so much.

It is impossible to omit mentioning the work of the redheaded Mary Slessor, who went to Calabar in the Niger delta area in 1876, leaving the festering slums of Scotland and the poverty brought on by an alcoholic father who begat a new baby every year. Before being overtaken by the colonial regimes, she did some remarkably fine work and continued it to her death in 1915. It was a marvelous moment when she prodded a potentate in the belly with her parasol and called him a "filthy polygamist" for trying to marry one of her sweet young female pupils. But her greatest triumph was her discouraging and stopping the killing of twin babies.

The work of such trailblazers was overtaken by the colonial fever that broke out in Europe. Livingstone was lucky enough to die in the heartland of the African bush. But both Freeman and Crowther were submitted to insult by accountants and efficiency experts who found their bookkeeping sadly lacking and accused their African helpers of corruption. (Teachers brought in from Sierra Leone and Gold Coast had been very poorly paid where congregational support had not yet developed, and had had to live on the propensities of their wives as traders and such facilities for profit as their position afforded.) The industrial revolution and the application of Darwin's ideas to theories of race and the survival of the fittest meant that newly arrived, highly trained strangers could sit in judgment of older, experienced workers in Africa. Before we describe the general onset and development of the colonial period, we must say something of the Islamic achievement in the nineteenth century, before the European takeover.

THE GREAT CENTURY OF MUSLIM THEOCRATS
AND HOLY WARRIORS

Muslim Reformers in Senegal and the Futa

In the far west, on the headwaters of the Rivers Senegal and Gambia and among the Futa highlands of Senegal and Guinea, the eighteenth-century Muslim reformers set up centers where God's will (as revealed in the Qur'an), the traditions, and the law were fully kept. The Fulani (Peul, Fulbe), who had wandered as nomads across Africa from the Senegal to Lake Chad, had produced learned and holy families of clerics who were in touch with reform movements in both Africa and the wider Islamic world. These clerics in other places besides the far west became aware of the laxity of the Muslims around them and of the vast numbers in their land still in the darkness.

Muslim Reformers in Northern Nigeria

In Hausaland and Kanem-Bornu in northern Nigeria, Islam had existed for centuries, but the reformers considered it in desperate need of reform and wider outreach. Shehu Usuman dan Fodio (Arabic—Sheikh Uthman ibn Fudi) arose to teach his people. Like the Prophet Muhammad, he met persecution from the local rulers. In 1804 he withdrew in an emigration (*hijra*) to purify and organize his followers, and he called on his still nomadic relatives for help. In the subsequent holy war (*jihād*), he and his relatives came to control an empire of 180,000 square miles and to insist that Islam of the highest quality should be maintained there. At the beginning of the twentieth century the British, with their policy of indirect rule, backed up the regimes of the remaining emirs, whose power has in some respects lasted into the modern Republic of Nigeria.

Other Nineteenth-Century Muslim Reformers and Warriors across Africa

The Shehu's reform was part of a much wider movement, but most of the others were much more clearly involved with resisting foreign encroachment, and with other aims besides reform. Umar ibn Said Tal from the Senegalese Futa, by the time of his death in 1864 or 1865, had created in the face of French intrusion of various kinds a sphere of influence that reached as far eastward as Timbuktu. Sheikh Ahmadu Bari of Macina (which lies north of Jenne) consolidated an area of God's rule that seems in many ways a utopia, but Al Hajj Umar thought fit to overcome it in 1862. In 1873 Samori Turi took Kankan, in what is now Guinea, and built up an empire stretching as far east as modern northern Ghana, before the French took the whole area in the 1890s. Listening to the oral tradition still circulating in Wa and Bole in northern Ghana, one is bound to wonder how much this hero, who terrorized not only the French army but millions of African women and children, was truly a man of God. Much depends on one's picture of God and heroism.

In the Sudan, a family of Turkish Albanian imperialists, along with various British and German mercenaries, pushed the rule of the nominally Muslim khedives up the Niles. Many Egyptians served in their forces, as well as Sudanic blacks in "Nubian" platoons. Slave-traders and other desperadoes followed in their wake. The mountains and jungles of Ethiopia held them upon one side, so they penetrated the other Nile to Buganda. The Dinka, the Acholi, and the Ganda felt their power in varying degrees. In the meantime, Swahili Muslims from the east coast had reached the Ganda area. In desperate reaction to the modernizing, secularizing, and Europeanizing of the khedives, the movement of the Sudanese Mahdi arose, gaining control of large parts of the Nile valley above Egypt during the last two decades of the nineteenth century. The Sudanese Mahdia, like a number of other Islamic movements of the time, had millenarian undertones: The new Islamic millenium was dawning, and a person chosen by Allah was to bring the righteous-ness and perfect rule of the New Age. Despite their admiration for the incomparable fighting qualities of their opponents, the British put down the movement with every resource of modern technology; but its spirit remained like that of other such movements, to contribute to the emer-gence of the new nations half a century later.

In the Horn of Africa in Somalia, among the people once led by Ah-mad Gran, the imperialists had to face from 1899 to 1920 the guerilla tactics of the mysterious person they called "the Mad Mahdi," Sayyid Muhammad Abdallah Hasan. Toward the end of the period the British used the tactic of obliterating towns and villages by aerial bombardment, after due notice and warning. The Islam of the Horn and the nationalism of Somalia owe a great debt to the Sayyid. But for a contribution to Islam out of all proportion, one must turn to the Muslims of the East African island of Zanzibar, to the little town of Bagamoyo on the mainland opposite, and to Lindi, a little farther down the coast.

Swahili Islam Goes Inland

Islam came very early to the East African coast, as we have already seen, but until the 1840s it had not penetrated far inland. Sayyid Said, the sultan of Muscat and Oman in southeastern Arabia, settled at Zan-zibar in those days and encouraged inland trade. Indian merchants and capitalists, mainly from Gujerat and working through Bombay, also came. The great caravan trails from Bagamoyo and Lindi were opened up, leading across Tanzania, as we call it today, to Lake Nyassa (Ma-lawi), to Lake Tanganyika, on to the waters of the Zaïre and its tributar-ies, and to the Great Lake (called Victoria by its European "discoverers," who followed in Swahili footsteps). From there they began to penetrate Buganda and move down the Nile to Acholiland.

The Africans who faced the incursion of the caravans recognized the traders as ruffians and desperadoes, with their firearms, slave-raiding, and massacres of elephants for ivory for the slaves to carry. Yet they somehow loved these traders, gave them wives, lands, and political power, and adopted some Swahili foods, methods of agriculture, and language. Above all, a gifted and faithful African minority took over and then mightily propagated the traders' Islam, which remained after the sultans of Zanzibar had been forgotten, Bagamoyo had shrunk to a village, and conquistadores like Tipoo Tib had gone home to enjoy their ill-gotten gains.

The Islam of the great warriors and reformers of West Africa, impor-tant and soul-stirring as it was, did not effectively penetrate to the heart of black Africa. Early in the century Islam tried to take over the Yoruba kingdom around Ilorin but failed for the moment. After a while, Mus-lims did achieve power in Ilorin, but then the rest of Yorubaland proved resistant. It was small groups of Muslims coming in from the Yoruba cities of the north, which had been broken up by slave-raiding and civil war, that brought Islam to the forest belt. Returning slaves who had held on to their Islam came back from Brazil or from resettlement in Sierra Leone to propagate Islam in Yoruba country.

The Precolonial Propagation of Islam: Some Examples

In Yoruba Country The Yoruba love of small, self-propagating, self-sustaining associations, their habit of allowing people to go their own way after they have been made aware of general opinion, permitted Islam to spread. Sometimes the Ifa oracle itself told certain individuals consulting it to become Muslim. Sometimes people joined out of admiration for the self-respect, universal outlook, and power of prayer and healing Islam gave. Some, hating colonialism and the cooperation Christianity appeared to give it, turned to Islam because of its reputation for opposing the Europeans. Above all, the fair might and greatness of Allah attracted many. At first they may not have been good Muslims, but after a generation or two they were second to none.

Among the Akan The Akan welcomed Muslims as traders and scribes, but as a nation they proved highly resistant to Islam. Perhaps this was because their own social and political structure survived intact until the present century, and Christianity more readily permitted them to retain their own institutions and basic beliefs, while giving them the Western education and technology that they desired.

Among Luo, the River and Lake Peoples In the southern Sudan and northern Uganda, the Dinka, Acholi, and Luo people as a whole did not take much to Islam, although certain prominent individuals did so. This may have been because during the regime of the khedives of Egypt and their penetration of Dinka and Luo lands, "lesser running dogs of the hated imperialists"[1] came to exploit and capture slaves and cattle, and these ruffians had identified themselves with Islam. Things were no better under the Sudanese Mahdi or during the interregnum before the British brought chaos to an end. When Christianity offered itself under the comparatively benevolent auspices of paternalistic British regimes, the Dinka and Luo joined in good numbers.

In Buganda In Buganda, the bringers of Islam to the kabaka's court in the 1840s were Swahili traders. The soldier Muslims coming up the Nile have been likened to fire, and the Swahili Muslims coming from the Indian Ocean to rain. They gained a secure base in Uganda. The recent military regime led by the self-styled General Amin was, in a way, a revival of the old soldierly Islam. Amin himself was a "Nubian," a member of the Muslim group descended from the Muslim soldiers

---

[1] A Chinese Marxist phrase adopted by educated Africans when referring to blacks cooperating with imperialists.

brought from farther down the Nile. The Ganda Muslims were not happy to be allied with him, but they remembered Lord Lugard's Maxim gun. Though Christian Acholi soldiers were singled out by Amin's thugs for massacre, Archbishop Janani Luwum, who was murdered by Amin, begged people not to think in terms of Christian versus Muslim or tribe versus tribe.

So far we have been dealing with the important precolonial period in the history of religions in Africa. We must now turn to the strange episode of the colonial takeover of Africa in the 1880s and 1890s. After that we will study the significance of the regaining of independence by the greater part of Africa from 1956 onwards. Finally, we will try to assess colonial influences on African religion, the rejection of colonialism, and the regaining of self-determination.

FROM COLONIALISM TO *UHURU* (FREEDOM)

Exploration and Occupation

The search for markets and for imperial glory, and the desire of some men to boss others—despite the protests of many who kept their heads—made some politicians in Europe scramble to dismember Africa. A continent still largely unexplored (that is, unknown to outsiders), Africa was divided up on paper by non-Africans meeting in Europe. By the end of the century only Liberia and Ethiopia were not in someone's empire, painted red, green, violet, or yellow on the map. The imperialists—British, Belgian, French, German, Portuguese, and Spanish, as well as white South Africans left by earlier Dutch-British adventures— thought in terms of "glory," "a place in the sun," "our task to civilize," "the need to raise darkest Africa to our level of enlightenment." For the Africans there was untold misery. The mother countries did not want to spend money on these overseas ventures. Before World War I, Togo (German) was one of the few colonial ventures that came near to breaking even. In the Congo, which a company dominated by King Leopold of Belgium ran at first, loads had to be head-portered; then a railway had to be built around the rapids on the great river. All of this had to be done by the wretched locals. Then wild rubber had to be collected to raise cash on the world market. New never-heard-of diseases and killers came. In some places the population was decimated, falling to one-tenth of its former level. Everywhere taxation had to be introduced to pay for "government." People who had lived full and self-sufficient lives had to be forced to take to a consumer cash economy. The mines and plantations needed the labor, and anyone who has been forced to sell his or her labor alone and far from home can guess what this meant in terms of human suffering.

Many Christians protested. Often, as in the case of the Congo atrocities, only their voices could effectively reach the world press. But Africa was being opened up, and it was impossible to go in or do anything without some relationship with the colonial governments. Being men of their time and needing every resource available, it was much easier for the Christians to cooperate than to keep shouting. If one wanted to help " the native" it was no use leaving it to others.

Colonial Policies toward Religions

The French Territories   In the vast French territories the French government was officially neutral in matters of religion. Since the days of the French Revolution, and with the rise of militant atheism in Europe, there was always a strong French voice calling for no religious nonsense. Yet the governments in France had in the main eventually come to terms with the Catholic Church. (French Protestants ever since 1685 have been few in number, though remarkably active.) It was immensely practical for the colonial governors to give the Church a fairly free hand, and especially to use her to provide western-style education at minimal cost to the government. Since the 1830s France had been occupying countries with large Muslim populations, from Tunisia and Algeria to Syria. Though at many points there had been fierce Islamic opposition, the colonial administrators found it useful to seek out Muslim individuals and vested interests who would cooperate and would use Islam as a means of building an empire. They were extremely chary of anything that might raise the cry "Islam in danger."

The Belgian and Portuguese Territories   The Swahili had brought Islam into the eastern part of the Belgian territories, and Islam had led opposition against the foreigners in the early days and remained under suspicion. English-speaking Protestants, especially Americans, gained a reputation for reporting to the world press; inevitably, great favor and resources were given to the Catholic Church, especially for education, so long as it cooperated and was staffed largely by nationals of the mother country. The situation in the Portuguese territories was similar, though there was little Islam in Angola.

South Africa   In the areas of British influence, South Africa is a special case, though there are analogies wherever there is a settler (as opposed to a colonial) regime. To the British tradition was added that of the Boer, the South African settler of Dutch background, and the tendency of settlers to see themselves as the chosen people occupying a land flowing with milk and honey and to stay away from or wipe out the tribes that have gone before them. In their attempt to preserve their regime, the whites have been willing to use and misuse anything, including religion. The churches have never stopped protesting, but at the same time they have to survive and work.

The British Territories   In British territories the governments declared noninterference with any religious practice, so long as it was not against the general principles of humanity and decency. At the beginning of this century, Queen Victoria had more Muslim subjects than the sultan of Turkey. Offences toward Muslims in Africa would soon be taken up in the Indian press. Moreover, Muslims were extremely useful in various ways. The families of the great Muslim rulers of northern Nigeria could be manipulated to cooperate in indirect rule. In return, Christian missionaries would be kept out. Using Muslim petty officials, policemen, interpreters, and clerks was much cheaper than importing Europeans, and less troublesome than Asians. Above all, the British had a great admiration for the manliness and self-respect Islam gave people. As far as Christianity was concerned, the British officials partook of the general Christian atmosphere that lurks in the background of British life. Missions were extremely useful for promoting education. Fair play between Catholics and Protestants was required by the British rules of fair play, though the play was often fairer to the Protestants. At the same time, Christianity could "spoil decent simple natives" and make spoiled ones "uppity." Accordingly, great areas where "the noble savage" could be himself with his traditional ways were sealed off from missionaries. Tom Mboya of Kenya dubbed this "the human zoo" approach.

German Policy   The Germans came comparatively late to the colonial game and were so fortunate as to be excluded early (during 1914–18). In Africa they are remembered as ruthless, but definite and principled within their own rules. As one old African gentleman told me near Masasi in old Tanganyika: "They had the belief that urinating in a certain small lake caused diseases among the villagers. They commanded not to do it. They shot one or two culprits. Some diseases disappeared from the lakeside." He obviously enjoyed telling a good yarn and pulling an academic's leg, but his admiration for the Germans was clear.

So it was with religion: If certain things that caused a nuisance could be prevented, people were left alone. Thus Muslims and traditionalists led the great revolt against the Germans in East Africa, and the Germans rapidly hanged the leading individuals concerned. But quite soon afterward Islam found itself able to spread; the Germans encouraged Muslims to serve in the lower ranks of the army and the administration because of the Muslims' literacy and knowledge of affairs. Christian missions could help develop the empire, and were allowed to operate along agreed-upon lines. In Germany the different churches had inherited definite areas; in the overseas empire each mission would be given a sphere of influence. Obviously, missions staffed by German speakers were preferable, but where there were established English-speaking groups, they would be tolerated.

Italy's Share of Empire   Italy, too, parts of which were freed from foreign colonization as late as 1870, developed colonial ambitions. She took over a portion of North Africa between British claims in Egypt and French claims in Tunisia and Algeria and called it Libya. At the southern end of the Red Sea she took over part of the African coast and called it Eritrea. Around the Horn of Africa she occupied Italian Somaliland, and in the mid-1930s she occupied Ethiopia. Mussolini, who had by this time taken over, had no real respect for religion, but he found it useful to put up a show of benevolence with regard to Islam in the coastal areas and, inland, to promote Roman Catholicism against the Ethiopian Orthodox Church. The Church was identified with the cause of Ethiopian independence as summed up in the person of Emperor Haile Selassie, who had been driven into exile. Early in World War II the British, using Indian troops, overran Eritrea and Ethiopia and gave them both to the emperor. Somalia they kept as a trust territory for a few more years.

While Ethiopia was under foreign yoke, the only part of Africa able to claim even nominal freedom from outside domination was Liberia; however, African scholars point out that even she remained under a certain United States remote control and that the rulers until recently were mainly American blacks and their descendants. These rulers were at times tied to ruthless and powerful foreign companies exploiting such products as rubber, iron, and bauxite. Despite this dismal situation created by outsiders, the religions prospered. Christian missions, mainly from America, were given a good deal of freedom to operate, Islam was able to flourish, and the African traditional religions were affected more by changing economic and social circumstance than by any official policies.

At the same time the life of the people in the inland villages retained much of the best of the old African scene, and in each period some eminent person connected with Liberia emerged onto the broader stage of international history. In 1851 Edward Wilmot Blyden, aged nineteen, migrated to Liberia, having been born on the Danish West Indian island of St. Thomas. He educated himself to the point where he was recognized as an eminent scholar, not only in Liberia but by the colonial governors of Sierra Leone and Nigeria. As a Christian minister he knew his Christianity excellently. He carefully studied Arabic and Islam, and came to view Islam as a religion enshrining something of the divine plan for Africa and the world, a concept that the greatest Christian theologians of the present are beginning to envision. His far-reaching views on self-determination by African Christians took some time to be worked out, but had considerable long-term effects. He died in 1912, never having reached the executive power his brilliance merited, because as the colonial period wore on, the white rulers of the British Empire were even less willing to trust people who had not come from Great Britain and had not gone to the "proper" schools.

Another great person connected with Liberia was William Wade Harris, who was born of indigenous stock around 1850. He fell foul of the police and was thrown in jail, where he had a vision in which God called him to preach. Around the age of sixty, he set off from Liberia, through the Ivory Coast toward Gold Coast/Ghana. Whole countrysides answered his call and awaited the coming of Christian teachers. By then it was 1915, and a jittery French colonial official quietly pushed him back into Liberia. Others continued the work, and the Harrisist Church has millions of followers, apart from the many who waited for teachers and were "picked up" by both Methodists and Catholics.

The High Noon of Colonialism

The period after immediate occupation, from the setting up of the colonial structure to the coming of independence, seems short in terms of world history for most parts of Africa—perhaps two generations, or the life of one old man or woman. For those who lived through it, it was interminable; then suddenly it was gone. An incredible amount was accomplished, much was obliterated, and many things changed, but the "inner head" of the people, as the Yoruba phrase it, was not destroyed. For the historian of religion, suddenly there is an overwhelming wealth and diversity of material. Besides the religious and governmental archives and the books that were published, there are the ephemeral sources: reports, mimeographed sheets, and newspaper articles that were meant to be, as is the Greek meaning of *ephemeral*, "but for the day," short-term. The camera begins to play a part, and oral material is still abundant.

The three main religious groups in Africa were forced to respond to the continuing Western intrusion. The traditionalists (which included many who were also Muslims and Christians) resisted in every way known, from large-scale armed warfare and years of guerilla leadership to positive nonviolence and emigration. But still the pervasive Westerner followed and tried to take over. It is particularly difficult to assess what part women played in the situation; they were undoubtedly the main conservers, yet we know that they were willing to experiment and innovate. Certainly the colonial officials and many of the missionaries and academic investigators found it hard to understand their role. It looked like a man's world, for society permitted males to come forward to take over education, technology, and leadership far more readily than it permitted women. In many places the new cash crops and economy were in male hands; a world population explosion and the increased difficulty of educating children demanded second thoughts on the issues of prolific childbearing and infertility. To summarize, people in Africa, including women who wanted to retain tradition and the ways of the mothers and fathers of old, displayed incredible resilience and the ability to think astutely and wisely, to keep alive the best in the spirit of the old until decisions could be made about the new.

For the Muslims, the main problem was to subject the incoming world of Western religion and secularism to Islamic principles. Thus if one wanted to "educate" one's child, that meant Western education, in which non-Islamic and anti-Islamic principles were rampant. Islam has nothing against science and technology. The Western theory on women's education—however far practice lagged behind—was that women should be given the same education as men. But the Muslim principle was that women were different from men and must be given their own space, their own opportunities to be themselves. Muslim views on discipline, sex, upbringing, prevention of antisocial and antifamilial activity, all differed from the views of the French, British, Belgian, Portuguese, and other educationalists who were busy introducing "education" in Africa. The world press and then American movies, world radio, and television all united to fill Africans with trepidation for their brothers and sisters in the West—so much so that African Muslims who took seriously the Qur'an's teaching on their special relationship to "the people of a Book" (for example, Jews and Christians) wondered whether Europeans and Americans were indeed different from those without religious knowledge, those who ignored their own sacred books and knew nothing of the Qur'an.

On the side of Africans who had become Christians, the problems were different. These people were prepared to accept a great deal of what the missionaries attached to Jesus Christ. But soon they learned to read their Bibles and they learned some Church history. Jesus was not a European; the Church, the Body of Christ, had passed through diverse cultures—Jewish, Greek, Roman, Germanic, and so on—and various features of these cultures had crept into Christianity. Jesus and his Church had not come to destroy the old but to fulfill it. African culture had not only a right to exist but a duty to perform, to contribute Africanness to the Body. The African Christian family became one of the most important focuses for the questioning that occurred during these years.

Traditionally, the African family is not merely wife, husband, and children, but the people on both sides related by blood and descent, the living of three or more generations, the dead, and the yet to be born. The basic woman-man relationship involves more than just two individuals, and more than sex: It includes members of various large corporate entities in every aspect of life. Sisterhood is powerful, and the wife belongs to womanhood as a group; she has her own status and independence and being; she is an individual expression of spirit-being at the level of Woman. Against this background the question was asked: What do we think about polygamy? (More correctly, in the African case it is called *polygyny*, the marriage of a number of women to one man.) In most cases in the rural agricultural setting where we studied this institution in Africa, it meant a number of separate but linked households run by individual wives who had a husband in common. In a situation where there was plenty of land, the man cleared the fields and did some of the heavier work. The women did most of the routine work and the storage and maintenance for their own households. At the same time there was usually an interdict on sexual intercourse from when pregnancy was known until after a mother stopped breast-feeding the child; this often occurred when the child was about two.

Divorce could be initiated by the man, but the woman's relatives and the community would try to bring about reconciliation. A woman could get her father's and mother's relatives to negotiate a divorce for her, and she could as a last resort pick up her children and belongings and go back to them. In either case the marriage guarantee ("bride-price") paid to her people would have to be discussed, and if necessary returned.

Within African Christianity the debate was fast and furious. On one side there were Africans who believed that, since the human male and female were made in the image of God, and since women and men were equal in the sight and love of God, then polygyny was against God's will. There were others who showed from the Old Testament that the patriarchs from Abraham onward had been polygynists, and that monogyny was a European ideal.

As ever, in Africa there were Christians who had definite rules and laws and those who said, like St. Augustine, the great African father, "Love and do as you like." In the meantime the outside world was closing in. World cash economics and land shortages made polygyny possible for only a very few rich people. Again, in the countries that Africans have thought of as having a Christian background, the European nations and America, divorce and marriage break-ups have increased so much that Christians everywhere are having to rethink basic principles.

Polygyny is still debated. The reader may wish to work out pros and cons and the implications for a wife and husband who try to come together in total, permanent, and exclusive self-giving, "until death us do part." Certainly the upshot is that Christians in Africa have a better body of material—from the Bible, theology, and the social sciences—to guide them on marriage, the family, the status of women, and children than most people elsewhere have. May they retain their leadership and assist others less fortunate.

THE INDEPENDENCE YEARS

Quite suddenly after World War II, the colonial powers (Germany and Italy being already gone) realized that they did not have forever in Africa. Even so, they were hardly ready when they had to leave, beginning in 1956. Some African countries had to wait until the 1970s, and the Africans of South Africa are still waiting. African traditional religion had played an important role in the first resistance movements when the foreign governors originally came. But these "revolts" had been ruthlessly put down, and leaders of traditional religion learned to keep a low profile. Nonetheless, African traditional religion remained alive not only to play an important part in the independence movement—for instance in Mau Mau, though the Kenyan mind is still divided on that movement—but to keep alive so much of the best of the old until it could be firmly established on the new. One of the worst features of colonialism (as Franz Fanon, the Caribbean psychiatrist, as well as various African novelists have pointed out) is what it causes the indigenous person to think of himself and of his fundamental characteristics. Too often the vociferous, the young, and the go-ahead have aped the outsider and despised their own people and their customs. Then comes the reverse stroke, when one utters a stream of words against the foreign while swallowing its worst features. Already Africans can look back on the colonial period—"a mere episode in our long history," as Dr. Nkrumah put it—and selectively retain features of African religion while rejecting a great deal of the sugary and plastic coming from outside.

According to Islam, religion and politics cannot be separated. Allah is directly concerned with the whole of life. Islam was able to develop an effective system by which certain leaders cooperated and became government pets, while the undertow of opposition never ceased. The Christians were in a difficult position. Their formal leadership was still to a great extent in foreign hands. Incredibly rapidly, indigenous leaders were found, and foreign financial and technical support was put on a brotherly basis. The Christians had also imported various theories from the West about the separation of church and state, and still had to think through for themselves the truly African Lordship of God in every facet of life. The greatest Christian contribution was perhaps the training ground that the churches provided for the civil servants and bureaucrats who had to run the newly independent states. The new politicians had in very many cases learned modern administrative and committee procedure from the Christians. Very many of them had also received their educations in Christian schools.

Some outstanding leaders such as Julius Nyerere and Kenneth Kaunda are devout Christians and have effectively used Gospel ideas of community and love in their political thinking and statements. (I doubt that either gentleman is pleased with all of the policies of the government he represents; both men want to serve all of their people loyally, including Muslims. Therefore, I am not about to identify their actions with Christianity.)

Marxism, Communism, and Socialism

Though British and European socialism had long been known in Africa, it was only during the independence period that Marxism, which as a secular ideology has deep religious connotations and certainly affects the religious systems around it, came to play a larger part in Africa than it previously had. Both Dr. Nkrumah of Ghana and Jomo Kenyatta of Kenya were just able to refute the colonial police's accusations that they were Communists. Both great leaders had undoubtedly studied Marxism deeply and used its ideas along with those of the traditional religion and Christianity they had studied, practiced, and knew so intimately.

Apart from a general ideological contribution, various Soviet, East German, Czech, Yugoslav, and Chinese aid projects have been completed. The Chinese railroad from Dar-es-Salaam to Zambia is a model of brotherly help. The donors gave out of their own poverty. As far as possible, local resources and appropriate technology were used, and then the helpers went home. During the last ten years governments have arisen in Ethiopia, Angola, and Mozambique that have owed a great deal to Communist military help. In Ethiopia, the Church once owned vast lands now confiscated; none of its leaders had been trained in the modern style, and it was identified with the traditional and with the emperor who was toppled from power in 1974. Yet the Ethiopian Church survives: Released from the chains of the past, it may awake to new life. In Angola and Mozambique, both of which achieved independence from Portugal in 1975, the Catholic Church has suffered for centuries by being too closely connected (and smothered) by Portuguese colonial power. Under the new regimes, which have shown Marxist tendencies, she has lost lands and privileges but gained freedom of the soul.

Marxist regimes can hit the traditional religions hard. In talking to official guides provided by Soviet and mainland Chinese tourist agencies, one gathers that there are no deliberate attacks. Indeed, if the religions can reappear as folklore and pretty peasant customs, they can get state patronage. But the pressure of state education and national service, and the need to spend time on communist projects and learning if one wants to get to the top, exert a steady pressure. Yet if one wants to be different and counter, if one wants to belong and to be related to one's roots, information from Siberia, Mongolia, and Tibet shows how well traditional religions can not only survive but spread. Whatever the reader may think of these possibilities, certainly Africa will make of Marxism something new. Religion has every reason to suspect and to survive all forms of materialism, be they dialectical or capitalist. Perhaps African Marxism will recognize and evoke yet new beauties in the three religions of Africa.

The Emergence of an African Christianity and Islam

During this century, a Christianity and Islam have emerged in Africa that are recognizably like their counterparts in other areas of the world but are also perceptibly and peculiarly African. On the Christian side, the difference can be summed up in one word: *Africanization*. The leadership is African: There are African cardinals, bishops, apostles, prophets. Outside religious authorities, where they exist, have to take African opinion very carefully into account. There is a concerted and conscious effort to Africanize liturgy, architecture, and music. Here is but one example, pertaining to the central matter of Bible study: At Kumasi in the Asante forest, within fifty years of the British takeover Akan students were retranslating the original Greek and Hebrew and rethinking Christian doctrine. In a period as short as fifty years, if one brings nothing else into the new world (and into Asante a great deal was brought, including social structure) one brings forms of thought. These include ways of expressing the love of God, the response of woman and man to that love, and the relationship of humans to the universe.

The Churches of African Initiative

This century has also seen the emergence on a colossal scale of the African independent churches. This is not to imply that the churches that have grown out of the missionary churches and have maintained full communion internationally are not independent or African, but to give a convenient label to groups claiming to be Christian that have resulted from African initiatives and have totally eschewed non-African leadership. The subject of the African independent churches demands a volume of its own. Here it must suffice to say that they vary from internationally recognized groups claiming millions of adherents—such as the Harrisist Church of the Ivory Coast, Liberia, and Ghana, or the Church founded by Simon Kimbangu in Zaïre—to house-churches that have gathered around a holy mother with powers of healing.

The Church of Simon Kimbangu Simon Kimbangu (1889–1951) grew up in the traffic and strife corridor at the mouth of the Congo/Zaïre, where for centuries the local people had suffered at the hands of the powers around them, especially the hands of the Portuguese and Belgians. Two centuries earlier Donna Beatrix had spoken out for a more indigenous Christianity. Simon began to teach Christianity as he understood it, the good news of a truly African Savior who demanded self-determination, the end of oppression, the sharing of resources, and the bringing of practical love to the needy. The Belgian colonial officials, backed by the ecclesiastical hierarchy, all loyal members of Belgian traditional Christianity, smelled mutiny and revolution in Kimbangu's teaching.

In 1921 it was decided to arrest and obliterate him. He forbade his people to take up arms, and he could have escaped. At about the same age as Jesus he went forward to his Passion. As he stood silently, he was sentenced to be scourged and put to death. Protestant missionaries, who felt that their Biblical teaching and militant hymns were partly responsible for Kimbangu's taking the Gospel message seriously, appealed to the Belgian king, who commuted the sentence to life imprisonment. Simon got his 120 lashes and uncomplainingly spent the next thirty years in prison, in solitary confinement or faithfully doing menial tasks in the prison kitchen. When independence came, his church had millions of members. The regime of President Mobutu has at times found this church valuable in a program of African "authenticity" that is carried on during the selling of the country's economic strength to outsiders. As of the time of this writing, the leaders of the church have avoided letting the church-state situation come full circle.

Why African Independent Churches? In an overwhelmingly voluminous literature, scholars have given many reasons for the rise of the African independent churches. Glancing back at the four main groups whose traditional religions we have studied, we find examples of most of the variables. In southern Ghana and southwestern Nigeria (Akan and Yoruba), independent churches have proliferated and flourished. In the southern Sudan and Uganda (Dinka, Acholi, and Ganda) they have not. But the Luo area of Kenya and the Kavirondo Gulf on the Great Lake seethe with them. (Assistance for deeper study is provided in the bibliography, for those who want it.) The one constant factor appears to be African spiritual exuberance, and whether or not it can express itself through the traditional international churches and in life in general. Many believe that because so much of Africa is now free, church activity will die down as politics, trade unions, and so on take over. So far, there is little sign of this.

The Africanity of African Islam

In asking in what ways African Islam is African—as opposed to other Islams that I have tried to study in Pakistan and India, or the Islam one reads about in Egypt, Saudi Arabia, or Iraq—I am struck dumb, because it is so hard to generalize. On one side there is the Muslim gentleman of Dakar, more French than many Frenchmen; on the other, there are the village Muslims of northern Nigeria or eastern Tanzania who are so close to the Punjabi Mussulman in their stolid, earthy goodness and decency. Let me speak of the young Nigerian, Ghanaian, and Ugandan Muslims I have gotten to know closely. They are very serious in their Islam. They know their Qur'an, the main ideas of *tafsīr* (exegesis), and the basic principles of the *sharīʿa*, the Muslim way of life. While they respect the Arabic, their knowledge has come mainly through English. They are strict about the great fast and the great festivals; they are serious about the prayers, and they give generously to Islam, though they are bewildered about the latest teaching on tithing and taking interest. As soon as possible, they gladly avail themselves of the cheap charter flights for pilgrims. Though those who go on the pilgrimage, like Malcolm X, return deeply impressed by the brotherhood of Islam, often they are not very happy about self-styled Islamic governments or wholesale public slaughtering of animals.

These Muslims have grown up in circumstances that do not permit any dreams of an Islamic state or society. They do not have a minority outlook, but welcome multiculturalism, secularism, and the presence of other religions. The status of women in their society is not like that of women in the West or in Arabia, yet no one can say that these women are in subjection or servitude any more than one can say that they run wild or are domineering. It appears that people like these Muslims will lead Islam into the next century. Their easy laughter, their dignity in testing the new, and their authentic roots in the past indeed make them the paladins of a new humanity.

The Three Religions in the Modern Situation

By examining the various colonial and independent governments' politics and attitudes toward religion, we have unearthed only some of the factors affecting religion in Africa during the colonial and independence periods, which in many places lasted little more than seventy years. The economic factors must also be taken into account—cash economy onward to incorporation in a world market run for the benefit of foreign countries. Here also the imposition of new methods of communication, the railroad, the Model T Ford, the VW bus, and aircraft, as well as "world languages" like French and English, printing, radio, and television, must be included. As forests were destroyed and plantations opened up, and as cities grew, the effects on social and ecology-based religions can be imagined. The effects upon that elusive entity "the soul of Africa" are more difficult to describe.

Despite the suffering, poverty, and underdevelopment imposed by foreign rule, during the independence era (the 1960s) hopes ran high, and religious people of all types were among the most optimistic. In Ghana, a church leader greeted the sixties as the decade of "God Has a New Africa—Ghana." There was a tremendous release of hope and genuine magnanimity, "greatness of heart, of mind." Thus the distinguished American black intellectual W. E. Du Bois (1868–1963) decided to spend his last years in Accra, Ghana. In the early sixties he gave generously of his time, to discuss with me the past and future of the black world. He spoke of his experiences as a black in the United States. He was full of hope that Africa's freedom would do much to secure fuller recognition of black rights. He felt sure that Africans would work with Asians and other oppressed peoples to take over world leadership and bring world affairs, especially in politics and economics, nearer to sanity and to the kind of constructive overall planning and mutual help that alone would save us from catastrophe. Twenty years later, to many Africans those optimistic dreams seem far away, and the future looms bleak.

Religious people, whether traditionalist, Christian, or Muslim, at all times take meaninglessness, despair, and hopelessness into account, but they cannot be overcome by them. Yet the friendly outside observer finds these ideas coming more and more into the conversation and writings of the African thinkers and writers with whom he shared the high hopes of the independence era. It is not only that South Africa remains in chains, but partly that time has run out, and the outside world—particularly the United States and Europe, for whom there remains immense respect as homes of the ideals of freedom and assistance to others—have failed to understand and help with Africa's real needs. Part of the problem is also that neo-colonialism continues to drain away resources; militarism and weapons go on increasing, while food decreases. One set of lunatic military men follows another in coup after coup. Politicians and potential leaders are more concerned with their own riches than with the plight of the poor. The obscene display of wealth and luxury flaunts itself in the face of starvation; the great ones can get the most expensive medical treatment in the world, while the children of the poor die for the lack of basic medicine. There have been cruel droughts, and if they go on millions will starve unless the outside world assists. Africa is facing one of the worst disasters in human history. Even so, in Africa there are women and men of religion who are thinking and working to bring true peace, joy, and plenty to Africa, and from there to all of us.

THE SURVIVAL OF THE AFRICAN TRADITIONAL RELIGIONS

What happened to African traditional religions? Were they destroyed? By no means. They live to contribute to world religion and civilization. This study, having covered many years of African religion, yields certain broad conclusions, which I shall try to summarize, however bitterly I regret the lack of space to go into detail.

Because our minds are obsessed with the large-scale and the uniform, we keep looking for the simplified system that will override and overleap all others. There have been moments in Africa when someone thought a messiah had arisen whose figure would overleap "tribal" language and cultural barriers, who would, through religion and ideology, project the true African personality. In some places a movement like Godianism, basing itself on an African theology and doctrine with all the aid of modern organization and publicity, has arisen and reached the rostrum of the United Nations, only to find its place with thousands of other denominations struggling to survive. African religion is more subtle than all this. The dancing, the festivals, the jollifications alone tell us to look deeper. African religions are trying to teach us precisely not to hanker after the big, the unitary, and the sweeping, but to appreciate the small, the human, and the homely—the homegrown product. The *Swadeshi* of Gandhian teaching—*Swaraj*, self-rule, self-regulation, self-determination, thence self-expression—are an analogy. The individual religious systems are tremendously tenacious and resilient, and they find ways of adapting. Cities are not new to them, nor are the basics of Western technology and science—trial and error, the use of hypothesis and experiment, the incorporation of new factors on a human scale.

These small units can and do work together and add up. Though we have talked of the religions of small groups of people and of the resultant remaking of Christianity and Islam, in this little book we have outlined the basic beliefs of over 200 million people.

Survival of African Traditional Religion through Christianity and Islam

Besides surviving in its own right, the African traditional religion will survive in many other ways, but especially through the Christianity and Islam it has shaped. If we briefly compare the headings of the paradigm we worked out for African traditional religion with their counterparts in Christianity and Islam, we will see some of the ways in which those religions have and will become vehicles for African traditional thought and practice. In a world Christianity dominated by European thought that has tended to evaporate God into a wordy abstraction, African Christian theologians will bring God closer to us. As Dr. J. S. Mbiti of Kenya once remarked, "European and American Christians put God in a box and perhaps peep at Him for a few minutes on Sunday morning; to us He is involved in every moment."

In international meetings of Christian theologians, the Latin Americans and United States blacks will speak much of liberation theology, of the Christ who frees from slavery and from racial and economic oppression and exploitation. Africans can obviously join this movement on equal terms. But they have much to add about an exemplary human being who became a mouthpiece and embodiment of divine spirit. They can think out the meeting of divine and human spirit in an incarnation, an indwelling of one in the other which is not a mere "enfleshment" (*carnis* is Latin for "flesh" or "body"), but a true "enhumanment"—thus getting back to the original early Church teaching in which *anthropos* was the word used. There is no partiality of meaning, no sexual imbalance in this point of view. Christianity is basically an "incarnational" religion. African religion, with the human at the center of an interrelated cosmos, has much to tell Christianity, and it can remind Christianity of the best in traditional Christian thought.

The Great Spirits—the *Òrìṣà*, the *'Nyame Baa*, the *Balubaale*—are also very much alive. They have crossed the water in the stinking holds of slave ships and have come to dwell among us and show their glory in Brazil, in Haiti, in Jamaica, and among some black congregations in the United States. They have contributed to the Pentecostal movement.

In regard to Islam, in some parts of the world people have so emphasized the oneness of Allah and his all-mightiness that they make Him remote, yet at the same time tacitly give almost dualistic power to Satan. An African Muslim thinks this matter through against his own background, both rejecting and affirming it. Satan is seen to be but a function of the principles of the universe, principles that come from God and that involve both nature and humanity. God is the ultimate criterion, however much spiritual powers, including those of the human being, may appear in certain circumstances to have an ultimacy of their own.

Another place where African Islam teaches us all concerns the doctrine of God. Some Muslim legalists seem to hand a God of love over to the Christians, even though every *sura* of the Qur'an except one begins by reminding us that Allah is compassionate and merciful. The African Muslim, because he often knows Christianity well and because life is too lively to be merely legalistic and judiciary, uses the power of Allah's love to reinforce the sense of brotherhood and sisterhood and of infinite compassion for all things, including the environment.

The Doctrine of the Human Being

We noted above that the Greek word for the human being, woman and man, is *anthropos*. European science has given the word a very specific meaning that cuts the study of the human being off from the study of God and the soul. African religion is willing to use Western methods of study, but insists that the human being be contemplated as including divine and spiritual elements. At the same time that the human being incorporates elements from the earth and the cosmos, she or he is not separate from animals, trees, and waters. The human being must not be seen as merely an individual particle but as part of a community and ultimately of a cosmic symphony of being. There is a divine principle—a power, force, and spirit in all things—that finds focus in the human being, that special creature who has essential tasks to fulfill.

The Ancestors and Ancestresses and the Impersonal Powers

The African veneration of the ancestors and ancestresses survives easily in the Christian teaching on the communion of saints and in Muslim reverence for the dead, the care of graves, and the services commemorating the dead. (We in the West who make our fathers into comic characters and inwardly deride our mothers—though we indulge in sentimental cults on certain days of the year—need to come to terms not only with our physical but our social inheritances.)

In looking at the lesser, impersonal powers and their manipulation (witchcraft, sorcery, charms, amulets, ordeals), we perceive a basic belief that the human being lives in a cosmos of spirit-powers, principles, and forces.

The Ecology of Spirit

The central search in African tradition is for wholeness of being and harmony with the powers. Medicine and surgery based on experience and experiment have their place, but the keeping of balance and the principles of right living are also important. To give an example of the application of this teaching in a world context, it is expedient to treat a cancer with surgery or with whatever therapy, more or less horrible, science at the moment prescribes, but it is also necessary to eradicate the types of pollution and radiation that make the cancer so common. Behind that pollution and radiation are the spiritual forces (dwelling also in and expressed by human minds and actions) that have rushed ahead with science and technology and development without stopping to consider the consequences.

African Divine Mysticism

In our paradigm we discussed African methods of communicating with the divine. There are many ways in which African Christian and Muslim prayer, festivals, fasting, pilgrimages, and rites of passage can and do continue elements of African traditional religion to the enrichment of all concerned. With regard to sacrifice, here are notes on a sermon preached one Holy Week in Rubaga Cathedral, Kampala, by the late Archbishop Joseph Kiwanuka:

> We Africans had many kinds of sacrificial offerings to God and the spirits. Some were for *pro*pitiation, that is, to gain favor. Some were for *ex*piation, to cover up our failures. Some for communion, to join in sharing. Christ took this all up in his one sacrifice on the cross. In the Mass the priest takes us to join in that great sacrifice. Thus in and through the Mass you may wipe away your sins, regain your place in the love and favor of God and join in fellowship with God, with the Blessed Mary Ever-Virgin and all the Saints and with the faithful at all times and in all the world. . . . Let us then go forward with the priest to that great offering.

Without creating incongruity, I can put beside this notes on an exposition given by the late Sheikh Ahmed, also of Kampala, during the Muslim great feast of sacrifice in the same year:

> Today in our minds we stand beside the pilgrims offering sacrifice near Mecca. They come from all over the world. We are proud of that, also of our own pilgrims whom we sent and hope soon by Allah's blessing to welcome back. They offer sacrifice for us and with us. We think back through our lives how with joy we have celebrated this festival. We think of the loved ones now departed who stood with us to rejoice and pray. We think of the future of the young ones with us now. All look to when our Lord and Master Muhammad offered this sacrifice, cleansed from the idolatry and wrong belief of those who had obscured the truth. He associated himself with the sacrifice of the Prophet Ibrahim when in obedience he was willing to offer even his son but God substituted a ram. Our people of former days, we ourselves were obscurers of the truth, but the truth of sacrifice is again made clear to us. Our whole life as Muslims is a giving and utter devotion to Allah.

While the sunlight gleams on African bodies and muscles, and laughter in the brilliance of African minds that relentlessly search out the truth, while the waters of the great rivers leap over rapids or emerge snarling from turbines, while the wild hornets swarm and the herds of great animals find their sustenance and the eternal snow-peaks jut out from the equator, the religions of Africa will live and teach first Africa, then through her the world, and human beings will take their appropriate place in the cosmos.

May Mungu, Kwoth, Olódùmarè, 'Nyame, God, and Allah be loving and merciful; may the Great Spirits bring only good; may the divine Essence that dwells in the trees, the rivers, the hills, and in human beings work healing and wholeness among us; may the cosmic powers of the universe and the lower world be harmonious for us. May the *sunsum* (soul) of Africa be cool. May we be forgiven all deviations and missings of the mark.

Bibliography

Full and annotated bibliographies of earlier material will be found in N. Q. King, *Religions of Africa* (New York: Harper & Row, 1970), and *Christian and Muslim in Africa* (New York: Harper & Row, 1971). The following bibliography confines itself mainly to material published since then that is readily available. The essential works, for those who are using this text as an introduction and have a minimum of time, are marked *. More advanced specialist material is marked †. General readers and those wanting to follow up a subject here and there should use works that are asterisked or unmarked.

BIBLIOGRAPHIES

The African Studies Association published Yvette Scheven's *Bibliographies for African Studies*,† 1970–75 and 1976–79 (Waltham, Mass.: 1977 and 1980). Ethel L. Williams and Clifton F. Brown's *The Howard University Bibliography of African and Afro-American Religious Studies with Locations in American Libraries*† (Wilmington, Del.: Scholarly Resources, 1977) is full of pleasant surprises. Patrick Ofori's *Black African Traditional Religions and Philosophy*† (Nendeln, Lichtenstein: Kraus-Thomson, 1975) usefully overlaps material earlier than the last ten years. The careful researcher will make systematic use of the International African Institute's great bibliography,† which goes back to 1929. In 1972 its compilation was taken over by the library of the School of Oriental and African Studies at the University of London. Since 1973 it has been published by Mansell

Publishing. Hans M. Zell's *African Books in Print*,[†] 2 vols. (London: Mansell, 1983) is also available.

ANTHROPOLOGICAL AND HISTORICAL BACKGROUND AND REFERENCE

The International African Institute's *Ethnographical Surveys*[†] continue to be published in London. There are now more than fifty volumes, covering most regions of Africa with a summary of data and a basic bibliography. The *Cambridge History of Africa*[†] (Cambridge: The University Press, 1978 and onward), edited by J. D. Fage, Roland Oliver, Michael Crowder, and others, is projected to be eight volumes, of which I have seen five. It has great quantities of material on religion, presented in the framework of history, together with exhaustive, humanely presented bibliographies. Additional insights can be gained by reference to J.F.A. Ajayi and Michael Crowder's two-volume *History of West Africa*[†] (New York: Columbia University Press, 1976 and 1973) and to the *Oxford History of East Africa*[†] and the *Oxford History of South Africa*[†]. The UNESCO *General History of Africa*,[†] published jointly by Heinemann of London and the University of California Press, Los Angeles, is to appear in eight volumes. Two volumes on methodology and prehistory and ancient civilizations were published in 1981. Vol. IV on the twelfth to sixteenth centuries appeared in 1984, and Vol. VII on the colonial period in 1985. These massive sets of volumes are a great monument to the fact that African history has emerged as a full academic subject during my lifetime. (Religious studies and histories of religion lag far behind.)

It partially remains for truly and fully indigenous schools of history to emerge. Nigeria, Kenya, and Tanzania seem to be leading, and others are coming up.

GENERAL BACKGROUND

Jean Hiernaux, *The People of Africa** (New York: Charles Scribner's Sons, 1974). Jacques Maquet, *Africanity, the Cultural Unity of Black Africa** (New York: Oxford University Press, 1972), and *Civilizations of Black Africa* (New York: Oxford University Press, 1972). Alpha I. Sow, Ola Balogun, Honorat Aguessy, and Pathé Diagne, *Introduction to African Culture, General Aspects** (Paris: UNESCO, 1979). An endless store of facts, figures, and bibliographies having to do with religion—including African traditional religion and Islam—will be found arranged country by country in David B. Barrett, ed., *World Christian Encyclopedia*[†] (Nairobi: Oxford University Press, 1982). While one knows that statistics can be notorious liars, and one mistrusts some theories of Church and Islamic growth, this book is essential to every serious researcher.

J. D. Fage's *An Atlas of African History** (London: 1978) can often be supplemented by regional atlases like the *Oxford Atlas for East Africa* (London: 1979) and country atlases like the *Uganda Atlas†* (Kampala, Uganda: 1962).

INTRODUCTIONS TO AFRICAN RELIGION

There are many books specially written to introduce Western students to the subject. Still unique, since it is by an African, stands Dr. John Mbiti's *African Religions and Philosophy** (New York: Doubleday, 1970). More recent introductions include Benjamin C. Ray, *African Religions: Symbol, Ritual and Community* (Englewood Cliffs, N.J.: Prentice-Hall, 1976), Robert Cameron Mitchell, *African Primal Religion* (Niles, Ill.: Argus Communications, 1977), Evan M. Zeusse, *Ritual Cosmos, the Sanctification of Life in African Religions* (Athens, Ohio: Ohio University Press, 1979), and Thomas E. Lawson, *Religions of Africa* (New York: Harper & Row, 1984).

WORKING BIBLIOGRAPHY TO THE CHAPTERS OF THIS BOOK

Chapter 1: The Yoruba

The religion of the Yoruba of Nigeria is well served by recent bibliographies like David E. Baldwin and Charlene M. Baldwin, *The Yoruba of Southwest Nigeria†* (Boston, Mass.: G. K. Hall, 1976). William Bascom was a pioneer of the modern study of his field. His *The Yoruba of Southwestern Nigeria** (New York: Holt, Rinehart and Winston, 1969) lays out the basic anthropological background. In a number of books, E. Geoffrey Parrinder developed the modern study of Yoruba religion, for example in *West African Religion*, originally published by Epworth Press of London (available in this country in a New York printing by Barnes & Noble, 1970). His Penguin book *Religion in Africa* (1969) is readily available. But the student may wish to go directly to E. Bolaji Idowu, *Olódùmarè, God in Yoruba Thought* (London: Longmans, 1962), and J. Ọmọṣade Awolalu, *Yoruba Beliefs and Sacrificial Rites** (London: Longmans, 1979); the latter is also available in paperback. Modupe Oduyoye, *The Sons of the Gods and the Daughters of Men* (Maryknoll, New York: Orbis Books, 1984) gives an Afro-Asiatic interpretation of Genesis, chapters 1–11, based securely on Yoruba thought.

It is important not to neglect poetry, folktales, dance, art, music, drama, the pamphlet press, and novels. The sheer ebullience and power of Yoruba life, which has religion at its heart, is hard to describe, but the nearest Yoruba student or Nigerian newspaper is a good way in. More and more material on special aspects of women's studies in Yorubaland is coming out. For now I will randomly suggest a few books, hoping that they are readily available worldwide. Henry J. Drewal and Margaret T. Drewal, *Gẹlẹdẹ, Art and Female Power among the Yoruba* (Bloomington: Indiana University Press, 1983), is supported by the film *Gelede* (twenty minutes, color, available from Indiana University). See also Judith Hoch-Smith, "Radical Yoruba Female Sexuality," in Judith Hoch-Smith and Anita Spring, eds., *Women in Ritual and Symbolic Roles* (New York: Plenum Press, 1978, pp. 245–67). Niara Sudarkasa, *Where Women Work: A Study of Yoruba Women in the Market Place and in the Home* (Ann Arbor: University of Michigan, 1973), has much to tell us besides economics. Ulli Beier, *Yoruba Myths** (Cambridge: University Press; New York: Crown Publishers, 1973). Robert D. Pelton's *The Trickster in West Africa*[†] (Berkeley and Los Angeles: 1980) is an excellent way into the theology of the folklore. For an outline and bibliography on sculpture, see William Fagg, *Yoruba Sculpture** (London: Collins, 1982).

As a topic for delightful research and pastime, I suggest Yoruba systems of geomancy and divination. There may be some primordial common basis for these as well as the main Bantu systems, the "Islamic" (that is, West Asian, Indian Ocean) *Ramli* sand divination, and perhaps the I-Ching! The connection between Africa and some New World black systems is too obvious to need mention. William Bascom, *Ifa Divination* (Bloomington: Indiana University Press, 1969). The same author—on a simpler system—*Sixteen Cowries: Yoruba Divination from Africa to the New World** (Bloomington: Indiana University Press, 1980). 'Wande Ambim-bọla's Ph.D. thesis has been published as *Ifa, an Exposition of Ifa Literary Corpus* (Ibadan: Oxford University Press, Nigeria, 1976). He published sixty-four complete poems in his *Ifa Divination Poetry* (New York: Nok Publishers, 1977). Judith Gleason's *A Recitation of Ifa* (New York: Grossman, 1973) gives a believer's point of view. A film entitled *Ifa: Yoruba Divination and Sacrifice* is also available from Indiana University (twenty minutes, black and white).

Reading novels with a religious bearing by African writers is a most enjoyable and effective method of study. Heinemann's African Writers Series covers the whole continent. Chinua Achebe came from southeastern Nigeria and suffered imprisonment under accusation of helping Biafra. His four novels* remain unsurpassed: *Things Fall Apart* (1958), *No Longer at Ease* (1960), *Arrow of God* (1964), and *A Man of the People* (1966). Gerald Moore's *Twelve African Writers* (London: Hutchinson, 1980) gives a good lead-in to the whole literature.

In regard to philosophy of religion, the Nigerian universities are very active, and glimpses of their thinking in an African context will be found in Robin Horton and Ruth Finnegan, eds., *Modes of Thought: Essays on Thinking in Western and Non-Western Societies** (London: Faber & Faber, 1973), and Ivan Karp and Charles S. Bird, eds., *Explorations in African Systems of Thought*[†] (Bloomington: Indiana University Press, 1980). On

the Ghanaian side, see Kwasi Wiredu, *Philosophy of an African Culture*
(Cambridge: 1980). Also important is E. A. Ruch and K. C. Anyanwu, *African Philosophy, an Introduction to the Main Philosophical Trends in Contemporary Africa* (Rome: Catholic Book Agency, 1981). Professor Ruch teaches at the National University of Lesotho and Dr. Anyanwa at the University of Lagos. Paulin J. Hountondji's *African Philosophy, Myth and Reality* (London: Hutchinson, 1983) expands certain elements especially of Francophone African Philosophy most helpfully.

Chapter 2: The Akan of Ghana

The Akan had the services not only of the Germans, Danes, and Swiss of the Basel Mission, but of a government anthropologist who fell in love with them and was a master of English prose. Captain R. S. Rattray's *Ashanti* (Oxford: Clarendon Press, 1923) and *Religion and Art in Ashanti* (London: Oxford University Press, 1927) are classics. His *Ashanti Proverbs* (London: Oxford University Press, 1916) is second-rate, but more accessible than the Baseler and local Twi collections that surpass it. The Akan also very early produced their own theologians writing in English. Dr. J. B. Danquah had a divine madness and genius for theological study. His *Akan Doctrine of God* (originally published in 1944; second edition prepared by Kwesi Dickson, London: 1968) should be read with respect for a masterpiece, not for pedantic academic nicety. Professor Kofi A. Busia, a man of the Bono (Akan) people, spent many hours teaching me. A truly inspired and inspiring teacher, too honest to be a good politician, he held chairs in sociology in Ghana and Holland. His *Position of the Chief in Akan Society*† (London: Oxford University Press, 1958) is still very helpful.

Kwabena Nketia is a musicologist of world renown. Reading his *Dirges of the Akan People* (originally privately published at Achimota, 1955) is valuable preparation for that event we all share; if edited and annotated by a Ghanaian theologian, this work could stand beside the Tibetan and Egyptian *Books of the Dead*. His *Music of Africa*† (New York: Norton, 1974) contains a most helpful discography and bibliography. On Ghanaian art, an Akan master who could also write excellent English was Kofi Antuban, whose *Ghana's Heritage of Culture* was published by Koehler and Ameland at Leipzig in East Germany in 1963. See also A.A.Y. Kyerematen, *Panoply of Ghana* (London: Longmans, Green, 1964). Emmanuel V. Asihene's *Understanding the Traditional Art of Ghana* (Rutherford, N.J: Fairleigh Dickinson University Press, 1978) may perhaps be accessible. In the art of folklore, Aesop's tortoise may have started his long slow journey from West Africa; the Akan Ananse the Spider and Br'er Rabbit may be closely related. One can begin with Peter Addo's *Ghana Folk-Tales* (New York: Exposition Press, 1968).

The Religion of the Gã of Ghana, a Side-Glance   Among the Akan live the Gã people. The Ghanaian capital is one of their five towns. Margaret Field, *Religion and Medicine of the Gã People* (London: Oxford University

Press, 1937), and her *Search for Security* (London: 1960; second printing Northwestern University Press, 1962; the latter printing includes Akan and Gã material) were written after she took medical and psychiatric qualifications. These two works stand as memorials to Gã life and thought, and to a Western woman of incredible doggedness who devoted her life to an African people. Marion Kilson's *Kpele Lala, Gã Religious Songs and Symbols** (Cambridge, Mass.: Harvard University Press, 1971) continues worthily in the tradition.

For an African's very useful overview and comparison of Akan and Yoruba views with his own Mende background, the doyen of Sierra Leonean theologians, Harry Sawyer, should be consulted. His *God: Ancestor or Creator?*[+] (London: Longmans, 1970) gives a lead-in. Anyone wishing to follow up his thought will find a complete list of his writings to that date in Mark E. Glasswell and Edward W. Fasholé-Luke, eds., *New Testament Christianity for Africa and the World, Essays in Honour of Harry Sawyer*[+] (London: S.P.C.K., 1974).

Chapter 3: The Bantu

On the religion of the Ganda, the missionary anthropologist John Roscoe's *The Baganda* (original 1911; second edition, London: Frank Cass, 1965) remains basic if only for its faithfulness to (one-sided) Ganda traditionalists like Sir Apolo Kagwa. Beside it stands the work of another missionary, Ruth B. Fisher's *Twilight Tales of the Black Baganda* (original 1912; reprinted with a preface by Merrick Posnansky, London: Frank Cass, 1970). The title was the publisher's and is almost totally wrong—the myths and legends come from the neighboring Nyoro area but apply to the Ganda. Margaret C. Faller's *The Eastern Lacustrine Bantu** (London: Ethnographical Survey of Africa, International African Institute, 1960) remains basic, though one has to update it bibliographically. Baganda scholars writing in English are not few, but in our field a great portion of their work has yet to reach the world community. *The Uganda Journal* and *Dini na Mila*, both published at Kampala, give a foretaste to those with access to them. Kagwa's material is being translated. In history, the writings of Dr. Semakula Kiwanuka and his colleagues are appearing—for example, *A History of Buganda to 1900*[+] (London: Longmans, Green, 1971; New York: Africana, 1972) and his translation of Apolo Kagwa's *Kings of Buganda* (Nairobi: East African Publishing House, 1971).

On the traditional African side of the religion of the Swahili people, a full and careful bibliography will be found in Mtoro bin Mwinyi Bakari's *Customs of the Swahili People** (Berkeley and Los Angeles: University of California Press, 1981).

Chapter 4: The Lake and River People

Regarding the "Nilotic" peoples—including the Dinka, Nuer, Shilluk of Sudan, Acholi of Uganda, and Luo of Kenya—two anthropological classics deal with their religion: Godfrey Lienhardt, *Divinity and Experience, the Religion of the Dinka** (Oxford: The Clarendon Press, 1961), and E. Evans-Pritchard, *The Nuer Religion** (Oxford: The Clarendon Press, 1956). Francis Madine Deng, a Dinka scholar, is a prolific writer. At least five of his books concern us: *The Dinka of the Sudan* (New York: Holt, Rinehart and Winston, 1972), *The Dinka and their Songs* (Oxford: Clarendon Press, 1973), *Dinka Folktales* (New York: Africana Publishing Company, 1974), *Africans of Two Worlds** (New Haven: Yale University Press, 1978), and *Dinka Cosmology* (London: Ithaca Press, 1980).

On the Acholi, see Okot P'Bitek, *Religion of the Central Luo** (Kampala: East African Literature Bureau, 1971). Among Okot P'Bitek's other works well worth reading are *African Religions in Western Scholarship* (Nairobi: East African Publishing House, 1970), *Song of Lawino* and *Song of Ocol** (Nairobi: East African Publishing House, 1970), and his essays, *Africa's Cultural Revolution*[†] (Nairobi: MacMillan, 1973). In a remarkable tour de force, Bruce Lincoln compares Maasai, Dinka, Nuer, and the old Iranians in *Priests, Warriors and Cattle*[†] (Los Angeles and Berkeley: University of California Press, 1981).

Chapter 5: Divine Fellowship

On African prayer, John S. Mbiti's *The Prayers of African Religion*[†] (London: S.P.C.K., 1975) and Aylward Shorter's *Prayer in the Religious Traditions of Africa** (London: Oxford University Press, 1975) indicate only a whisper of its voice and the outskirts of its way. On the veneration of ancestors and ancestresses, William H. Newell, ed., *The Ancestors*[†] (The Hague: Mouton, 1976), will give a lead-in on a world scale.

On spirit possession and mediumship, Irving I. Zaretsky's *Bibliography*[†] on the topic has been republished by Garland Press, New York, in 1974. See also I. M. Lewis's *Ecstatic Religion, an Anthropological Study of Spirit Possession and Shamanism** (Baltimore: Penguin Books, 1971). On witchcraft, see Mary Douglas, ed., *Witchcraft: Accusations and Confessions* (London: Tavistock, 1971). On the topic of sacrifice, the classic is H. Hubert and M. Mauss, *Sacrifice, Its Nature and Function* (French original 1898; English translation published in London: Cohen and West, 1964). A very interesting discussion and up-to-date bibliography will be found in M.F.C. Bourdillon and Meyer Fortes, *Sacrifice* (London: Academic Press, 1980). We have mentioned Dr. Awolalu's book *Yoruba Religion and Sacrifice.** Beside it one can place Francis A. Arinze, *Sacrifice in Ibo Religion* (Ibadan, Nigeria: University Press, 1970). It, too, is positive and affirmative in its attitude; significantly, Arinze is a Roman Catholic archbishop and Awolalu a canon in the Church of Nigeria. (Dr. Idowu is patriarch of the Methodist Church in Nigeria.)

On religion at life's turning points (the rites of passage—birth, adolescence, marriage, and death), Victor W. Turner's masterworks still stand eminent: *The Forest of Symbols* (Ithaca: Cornell University Press, 1967), *The Drums of Affliction** (Oxford: Clarendon Press, 1968), and *The Ritual*

*Process** (Chicago: Aldine, 1969). *Revelation and Divination* (Ithaca: Cornell University Press, 1975) is now added.

On women's studies in Africa, an adequate account of woman's place in traditional religion is badly needed. Mercy Amba Oduyoye, a Ghanaian theologian working in Nigeria and overseas for the World Council of Churches, may produce it. Pioneer works like Audrey I. Richards, *Chisungu** (London: Faber and Faber, 1956), and Denise Paulme, ed., *Women of Tropical Africa* (Berkeley and Los Angeles: University of California Press, 1960), have led to works like Nancy J. Hafkin and Edna G. Bray, eds., *Women in Africa** (Stanford: University Press, 1976), and Christine Obbo, *African Women, Their Struggle for Economic Independence* (London: Zed Press, 1980). Browsing in the works of scholars like Lucy Mair, Laura Bohanan, Audrey Richards, and Mary Douglas can teach one a great deal.

On the religious studies side of the subject, some idea of the quickly advancing cutting edge can be gained in chapters relevant to Africa in collective works such as Jean S. La Fontaine, ed., *The Interpretation of Ritual: Essays in Honour of Audrey Richards* (London: Tavistock, 1972), Judith Plaskow and Joan Arnold Romero, eds., *Women and Religion* (Missoula, Mont.: American Academy of Religion and Scholars' Press, 1974), Rita M. Goss, ed., *Beyond Androcentrism* (Missoula, Mont.: Scholars' Press, 1977), Carol Christ and Judith Plaskow, eds., *Womanspirit Rising: A Feminist Reader in Religion* (San Francisco: Harper & Row, 1979), Rita Goss and Nancy Auer Falk, eds., *Unspoken Worlds: Women's Religious Lives in Non-Western Cultures* (San Francisco: Harper & Row, 1980), and Pat Holden, ed., *Women's Religious Experience* (Totowa, N.J.: Barnes & Noble, 1983). The literature in periodicals is also impressive; for guidance see Marion Kilson, "Women in Traditional African Religions" *(Journal of Religion in Africa* 8 (1976): 133–43), and Margaret Strobel, "African Women" *(Signs, Journal of Women in Culture and Society* 8 (1982): 109–31).

An enumeration of facts and some statement of the implications of the so-called "female circumcisions" may be studied in the report edited by Scilla McLean, *Female Circumcision, Excision and Infibulation* (London: Minorities Rights Group, 1980). See also Mary Daly, *Gyn/Ecology, the Metaethics of Radical Feminism* (Boston: Beacon Press, 1978).

In conclusion, on the religious status of women in Africa one can only say that using an annotated list like Laura Kratochvil's *African Women: a Select Bibliography†* (Cambridge, England: African Studies Centre, 1975) is much easier than consulting, for instance, the UNESCO or Library of Congress cumulative and accessions bibliographies under "Africa" and "Women" for the last decades, though a researcher who wants a full recovery of information must correlate information retrieved under the two topics.

Chapters 6 and 7

On the study of Christianity and Islam in Africa, their relationship to one another and to African traditional religion, one of the few books is

Noel King's *Christian and Muslim in Africa** (New York: Harper and Row, 1971). It was met with some amused chuckles, then silence. Its bibliographic essays, laid out country by country and period by period, will serve to 1971. To follow this up the student may study Islam and Christianity treated each by itself in the relevant volumes of the histories and bibliographies mentioned in the general section and then carry out the comparative study. W. Montgomery Watt's *Islam and Christianity Today* (London: Routledge and Kegan Paul, 1983) can guide with material and method. On Christianity, Adrian Hastings, *A History of African Christianity, 1950–1975** (Cambridge, England: University Press 1979), and Edward Fasholé-Luke, Richard Gray, Adrian Hastings, and Godwin Tasie, eds., *Christianity in Independent Africa* (Ibadan, Nigeria: Ibadan University Press, and London: Rex Collings, 1978), will bring things near the present.

The scholar wishing to go further will find Andrew Walls's regular bibliographical contributions to the *International Review of Missions*† (published at Geneva by the World Council of Churches) and Patrick E. Ofori's *Christianity in Tropical Africa: A Selective Annotated Bibliography* (Nendeln, Lichtenstein: KTO Press, 1977) most helpful. The African independent churches are now treated in Harold W. Turner's *Bibliography of New Religious Movements in Primal Societies*, vol. 1, *Black Africa*† (Boston, Mass.: G. K. Hall, 1977). A recent contribution to this field of study by an African is J. Akinyele Omoyajowo, *Cherubim and Seraphim, the History of an African Independent Church* (New York: Nok Publishers, 1982). On Islam, I. M. Lewis's updated edition of *Islam in Tropical Africa** (London: International African Institute, and Bloomington: Indiana University Press, 1980) brings things near to the present. Nehemia Levtzion's *Ancient Ghana and Mali* (London: Methuen, 1973) tells the story of those two kingdoms in medieval times. Peter B. Clarke, *West Africa and Islam* (London: Arnold and Co., 1982), gives a good summary. J. R. Willis is editing a series of studies by acknowledged experts called *West African Islamic History*. I have seen the first volume, *The Cultivators of Islam*† (London: Cass & Son, 1979). Lamin O. Sanneh's *The Jakhanke*† (London: International African Institute, 1979) is a highly technical book, but important because it indicates that first-class African scholars of Islam and Christianity writing in English are appearing. His *West African Christianity, the Religious Impact** (New York: Orbis Books, 1983) we hope signals the rise of a great new star on the horizon.

On some aspects of the Islamic brotherhoods, see Donal B. Cruise O'Brien, *The Mourides of Senegal, the Political and Economic Organization of an Islamic Brotherhood*† (London: Oxford University Press, 1971), and B. G. Martin, *Muslim Brotherhoods in the Nineteenth Century*† (Cambridge: University Press, 1976). A. H. Nimtz, *Islam and Politics in East Africa, the Sufi Order in Tanzania*† (Minneapolis: University of Minnesota Press, 1980), is especially strong on these groups in the Swahili heartlands. Louis Brenner's *West African Sufi* (Berkeley and Los Angeles: 1984) has recently appeared. Mary Smith's *Baba of Karo, a Woman of the Muslim*

Hausa (London: Faber & Faber, 1954) remains a classic. René A. Bravman's *Islam and Tribal Art in West Africa* (Cambridge: University Press, 1974) dispels some widely held presuppositions about alleged Islamic enmity to traditional art.

The research scholar may supplement these books by consulting Patrick E. Ofori's *Islam in Africa South of the Sahara*[†] (Nendeln, Lichtenstein: KTO Press, 1977) and Samir Zoghby's *Islam in Sub-Saharan Africa, a Partially Annotated Guide*[†] (Washington, D.C.: Library of Congress, 1978).

The Meeting and Interaction of the Three Religions among Selected Groups [·]
We used the Yoruba and Akan, the Dinka and Acholi, the Ganda and Swahili as our basic systems for study. Here are a few notable books that will help those who want to go into greater detail on the history and meeting of traditional religions, Christianity, and Islam among those peoples and in the nations to which they now belong. The background to our study of Christianity in the early days of Nigeria may be pursued in a more specialized way in J.F.A. Ajayi's *Christian Missions in Nigeria 1841–1891* (London: Longmans, 1965), E. A. Ayandele's *The Missionary Impact on Modern Nigeria 1842–1914* (London: Longmans, 1966), F. K. Ekechi's *Missionary Enterprise and Rivalry in Igboland, 1897–1914*[†] (London: Frank Cass, 1972), and James B. Webster's *The African Churches among the Yoruba, 1888–1922* (Oxford: Clarendon Press, 1964). The middle period may be studied in volume 2 of the *History of West Africa*,[†] edited by Ajayi and Crowder, and volumes 3 and 4 of C. P. Groves, *The Planting of Christianity in Africa*[†] (London: Lutterworth, 1948–58). Modern times may be studied in Adrian Hastings's *A History of African Christianity, 1950–1975* (Cambridge, England: University Press, 1979). His *African Christianity*[*] (London: Geoffrey Chapman, 1976) tries to interpret the history of the last century in less detail. Elizabeth Isichei, ed., *Varieties of Christian Experience in Nigeria* (London: Macmillan, 1982), and Walter L. Williams, *Black Americans and the Evangelization of Africa* (Madison: University of Wisconsin Press, 1982) are also relevant. Regarding Christianity and Islam among the Yoruba and in Nigeria, two Ph.D. theses have appeared in print: T.G.O. Gbadamosi's *The Growth of Islam among the Yoruba, 1841–1908*[*] (London: Longmans, 1978) and Patrick J. Ryan, *Imale: Yoruba Participation in the Muslim Tradition* (Missoula, Mont.: Scholars' Press, 1978). Between them, and with such works as Mervyn Hiskett's *The Sword of Truth, the Life and Times of Shehu Usuman dan Fodio* (New York: Oxford University Press, 1973) and his *Development of Islam in West Africa* (London: Longmans, 1982), the student will find a way ahead with Islam.

Turning to Ghana, F. L. Bartels, *The Roots of Ghana Methodism* (Cambridge, England: University Press, 1965), remains one of the outstanding works in church history by a Ghanaian. In some respects one can place beside it Kwesi Dickson's edition of S. G. Williamson's *Akan Religion and the Christian Faith, a Comparative Study of the Impact of Two Reli-*

gions (Accra: Ghana University Press, 1965). Two notable works in theology and the independent churches are John S. Pobee, *Toward an African Theology** (Nashville, Tenn.: Abingdon, 1979), and C. G. Baeta, *Prophetism in Ghana** (London: S.C.M. Press, 1962). In some sense Robert W. Wyllie's *Spiritism in Ghana: A Study of New Religious Movements*† (Missoula, Mont.: Scholars' Press, 1980) brings Baeta's pioneer study toward the present. Again, Hastings's *History of African Christianity* carries the whole story forward to 1975.

Islam has not spread as widely in Ghana as elsewhere. Its fortunes in the north can be studied in Nehemia Levitzion's *Muslims and Chiefs* (London: Oxford University Press, 1968). In Asante, Ivor Wilks tells the Islamic story in his essay in I. M. Lewis, ed., *Islam in Tropical Africa* (London: International African Institute, 1980). The history of Islam in the towns and *zongos* (strangers' quarters) of the south has yet to be gathered into a coordinated whole.

The coming of Islam and Christianity to the Dinka and their neighbors may be followed up in J. Spencer Trimingham's *Islam in the Sudan* (London: Oxford University Press, 1949) and C. P. Groves's *Planting of Christianity in Africa*, vols. 3 and 4. P. M. Holt, *The Mahdist State in the Sudan* (London: Oxford University Press, 1977), and P. M. Holt and M. W. Daly, *The History of the Sudan* (London: Wiedenfield & Nicholson, 1980), give historical background. These books and those of Adrian Hastings and Francis Mading Deng cited earlier provide many details. Independent African churches have developed little among the Dinka and their neighbors. The confluence of the three religions among the Acholi of Uganda and the Luo of Kenya may be studied in the books cited for those countries below.

For Kenya, it is best if possible to begin with David B. Barrett, ed., *Kenya Churches Handbook, the Development of Kenyan Christianity 1498–1973* (Kisumu, Kenya: Evangel Press, 1973). By use of its extensive bibliography, one can research the amazing proliferation of independent churches among the southern Luo. Kenya now has indigenous historians of mission: A. J. Temu, *British Protestant Missions* (London: Longmans, 1972) deals with the mainline Protestant situation to 1929. The story can be supplemented by Robert W. Strayer's *The Making of Mission Communities in East Africa* (London: Heinemann; Albany, N.Y.: S.U.N.Y. Press, 1978). Kenya has also produced notable Christian theologians. First there is Reverend Dr. J. S. Mbiti, *New Testament Eschatology in an African Background, a Study of the Encounter Between New Testament Theology and African Traditional Concepts** (London: Oxford University Press, 1971), and his *Concepts of God in Africa* (London: S.P.C.K., 1970). To my mind, the hard-hitting evangelical Byang H. Kato showed the utmost promise, but he was drowned in the ocean at Mombasa. Only his *Theological Pitfalls in Africa* (Kisumu, Kenya: Kenya Evangelical Publishing House, 1975) has reached me in print.

The Gaba Pastoral Institute has moved to Eldoret in Kenya. It is run by religious men and women from East Africa and elsewhere. A periodical published there, *The African Ecclesiastical Review (A.F.E.R.)*, takes up many problems affecting all the religions—rapid social change and the development of theology, marriage, and initiation in the new Africa. One of its employees is Dr. Aylward Shorter, who speaks the local languages and has lived in Africa for years. Stimulated by his African co-workers, he acts as a mouthpiece for the general discussion and intellectual cross-fertilization going on, and he has published a number of books. These include *African Culture and the Christian Church** (1973), *African Christian Theology* (1975), and *Priest in the Village* (1979). All were published by Geoffrey Chapman at Dublin and London.

For Uganda, M. Louise Pirouet's *Black Evangelists, the Spread of Christianity in Uganda, 1891–1914* (London: Rex Collings, 1978) tells of the early days. Fred B. Welbourn's *East African Christian** (London: Oxford University Press, 1965) takes the story forward, and Hastings's *History* and the *Oxford History of East Africa* bring it to the present. Orbis Books of Maryknoll, New York, are publishing a number of important books on African theology side by side with sister works on Latin American and American black theology. At press time only Kwesi A. Dickson's *Theology in Africa* (Maryknoll, N.Y.: Orbis Books, 1984) has reached me. At least four other titles announced promise to be equally important to the understanding of Christianity in Africa.

A number of Gandan theologians have been deeply influenced by the philosophy of Muntu (the human being) first set out by Father Placide Tempels in his *Bantu Philosophy* (originally written in Flemish). The earliest French translation I have seen was published at Elisabethville (Lubumbashi), Zaïre, in 1945. The English translation in a *Présence Africaine** edition (1959) is readily available. The ideas were popularized in Europe by Janheinz Jahn. Many East African scholars read French and carefully follow the thought of Alexis Kagamé, who is not far away across the mountains in Rwanda, as well as that of the philosophers of the *Présence Africaine* and Kinshasa schools. These most important intellectual movements are not yet well represented in English. Because of the traditions of the two churches in Uganda—the Roman Catholic of White Father background and the Anglican of Church Missionary Society background—there is a tradition to Africanize and indigenize. The incarnational thought of Cardinal Lavigerie and Henry Venn and its working out in Uganda have yet to be written up in one volume; perhaps this volume will come to us from the ashes of Amin's regime as Makerere University takes its new phoenix wings.

Islam in Uganda and in East Africa as a whole may be studied through J. Spencer Trimingham, *Islam in East Africa** (London: Oxford University Press, 1964), Abdu Kasozi, Arye Oded, and Noel King, *Islam and the Confluence of Religions in Uganda, 1840–1940*† (Tallahassee, Fla.: American Academy of Religion, 1972), Mtoro bin Mwinyi Bakari, *Customs of the Swahili** (Berkeley and Los Angeles: University of California Press, 1981), Ann P. Caplan, *Choice and Constraint in a Swahili Community*† (London:

Oxford University Press, 1975), and Margaret Strobel, *Muslim Women in Mombasa, 1890–1975* (New Haven: Yale University Press, 1979).

Christine Obbo, *African Women, Their Struggle for Economic Independence* (London: Zed Press, 1980), is ostensibly about women grappling with the economic situation in Kampala (Uganda) in the early 1970s, but it tells much about religion and women across Africa. The fate of Islam, Christianity, and traditional religions during the Amin years and the recovery from those years have yet to be fully written up, but see Akiiki B. Mujaju, "The Political Crisis of Church Institutions in Uganda" (*African Affairs*, 1976, vol. 75, pp. 67–85).

No readily available history of Christianity in Tanzania has appeared abroad recently, but Terence O. Ranger's *The African Churches of Tanzania* (Dar-es-Salaam: Historical Association of Tanzania, 1969) and his chapter "Christian Independency in Tanzania" in David Barrett's *African Initiatives in Religion* (Nairobi: East African Publishing House, 1971), if obtainable, are fundamental.

On Christian political leadership in Africa, the student may be interested in analyzing the religious content of Mwalimu Julius Nyerere's thought, beginning with the Arusha Declaration and *Man and Development* (Oxford: University Press, 1974). David Westerlund's *Ujamaa na dini, Some Aspects of Society and Religion in Tanzania, 1961–1977*[+] (Stockholm: Almquist and Wiksell, 1980) gives excellent background.

This bibliography is concerned only with books in English. We have concentrated upon four large areas, from west to east in equatorial Africa, in the hope of focusing a few beams of light rather than seeking an overall dim glow. However, the reader is strongly encouraged to go outside these geographical and linguistic limits to pursue any of the themes we have introduced. For deeper study of Central Africa—that is, the modern countries of Cameroun, the Central African Republic, Gabon, Congo, Zaïre, Angola, Malawi, Zambia, Zimbabwe, and Mozambique, a vast area which is 80 percent Bantu-speaking—consult David Birmingham and Phyllis M. Martin, eds., *History of Central Africa*, 2 vols. (London and New York: Longmans, 1983), together with the few books that follow. James W. Fernandez, *Bwiti, an Ethnography of the Religious Imagination in Africa* (Princeton: University Press, 1982), is a detailed study of a Fang group, the Fang being one of the peoples with the most highly developed metaphysics in Africa. T. Ranger and J. Weller, *Themes in the Christian History of Central Africa* (London: Heinemann, 1975). Ian Linden's *Catholics, Peasants and Chewa Resistance in Nyasaland* (London: Heinemann, 1974) and *The Catholic Church and the Struggle for Zimbabwe* (London, Longmans, 1980). M. L. Daneel, *The God of the Matopo Hills* (The Hague: Mouton, 1970). Gabriel Setiloane, *The Image of God among the Sotho-Tswana* (Rotterdam: A. A. Balkema, 1976). Michael Boudillon, *The Shona Peoples, an Ethnography with Special Reference to Religion* (Gweru, Zimbabwe: Mambo Press, 1976).

On the independent African churches in the vast areas that this book has not covered, see Gordon M. Haliburton's *The Prophet Harris* (London: Longmans, 1971), which tells of an apostolic African Christian and a mass movement in the former French Ivory Coast as well as in the British Gold Coast and Liberia during World War I. See also Sheila Walker's *The Religious Revolution in the Ivory Coast: The Prophet Harris and the Harrisist Church* (Chapel Hill: University of North Carolina Press, 1982). Marie-Louise Martin, *Kimbangu, an African Prophet and His Church* (Oxford: Basil Blackwell, 1971), gives the story of one of the greatest men and churches of Zaïre. The doyen of these studies, Bengt Sundkler, published his *Zulu Zion** (London: Oxford University Press) in 1976.

Michael G. Whisson and Martin West, eds., *Religion and Social Change in Southern Africa* (Cape Town: David Philip, and London: Rex Collings, 1975), and Marjorie Hope and James Young, *The South African Churches in a Revolutionary Situation* (Maryknoll, N.Y.: Orbis Books, 1981), will also greatly help a student wanting to learn where the religions of South Africa are going. Axel-Ivar Berglund, *Zulu Thought-Patterns and Symbolism* (London: C. Hurst, 1975), and Janet Hodgson, *The God of the Xhosa* (Cape Town: Oxford University Press, 1983), provide a valuable survey of parts of the traditional background. Translations from the French include Dominique Zahn's *The Religion, Spirituality and Thought of Traditional Africa* (Chicago: University of Chicago Press, 1979). Her little book *The Bambara* appeared in 1974 in Brill of Leiden's *Iconography of Religions* series. Jean Laude's *African Art of the Dogon* (New York: Dutton, 1973) opens up the amazing world of the African Dogon philosophies and cosmologists, but see also the Oxford University Press paperback by Marcel Griaule, *Conversations with Ogotemmeli** (1975), for the Carlos Castaneda and Don Juan of the African religious world. Lastly, the old Burgundian middle-European dream of kingship finds new life in the Congo in Luc de Heusch's *The Drunken King* (Bloomington: Indiana University Press, 1982).

There are some other topics that I have deliberately not touched and that the "do-it-yourself" student will find most rewarding and comparatively easy to follow up. One example is the San peoples, the so-called "Bushman" people of South Africa. Their remarkable lack of mindless aggression and violence and their ideas on fullness of life and euthanasia have much to offer us all. G. Silberbauer, *Hunter and Habitat in the Central Kalahari Desert* (Cambridge: University Press, 1981), and Richard Katz, *Boiling Energy, Community Healing among the Kalahari !Kung* (Cambridge, Mass.: Harvard University Press, 1982), give a useful bibliographical lead-in to the large amount of printed and filmed material available. The Marshall family's contribution to the material is outstanding.

As a complement and contrast to the Yoruba religion, a student will find it rewarding to read about the religion of the 12 million Igbo of eastern Nigeria. A good place to begin is with Dr. Emefie I. Metuk's *God and Man in African Religion* (London: Geoffrey Chapman, 1981) and his bibliography. However, remember to add the works of the novelist Chinua Achebe mentioned above, for the Igbo are his people.

Black African traditional religion is part of a world black movement. As a person with some Dravidian ancestry, I regret I have said nothing about the primordial oneness of African religion with some aspects of religion in parts of India, Southeast Asia, Melanesia, and aboriginal Australia. In the American context, the student should try to follow up with a study of the religion of the African diaspora (the seed scattered abroad) in the Americas. Here are a few titles to start the process. Ethel L. Williams and Clifton L. Brown, *Afro-American Studies, a Comprehensive Bibliography with Locations in American Libraries*† (Metuchen, N.J.: Scarecrow Press, 1972), St. Clair Drake, *The Redemption of Africa and Black Religion* (Chicago: Third World Press, 1971), Martin L. Kilson and Robert I. Rotberg, eds., *The African Diaspora, Interpretative Essays* (Cambridge, Mass.: Harvard University Press, 1976), George E. Simpson, *Black Religions in the New World* (New York: Columbia University Press, 1978). From them the reader may go into more detailed studies of particular themes or areas, for instance Roger Bastide, *The African Religions of Brazil** (Baltimore and London: Johns Hopkins University Press, 1978).There are also the various works of Leonard E. Barrett, a man with a Jamaican background, including *The Rastafarians** (Kingston and London: Sangster and Heinemann, 1967), Leslie B. Rout, *The African Experience in Spanish America* (Cambridge, England: The University Press, 1976), and Sheila S. Walker, *Ceremonial Spirit Possession in Africa and Afro-America* (Leiden: Brill, 1972).

ART, MUSIC, THE DANCE, AND DISCOGRAPHY, SLIDE LIBRARIES, AND MUSEUM CRAWLING

To sense fully the spirit of the African religions, they must be approached in their full panoply of nature, society, color, form, movement, music, song, and dance. Individual items in this total ecology, or a few of them at once, can be taken up by the student dwelling far away. There are museums and Africana collections within reach of most of us. Long hours, whole days, should be spent exploring these. As preparation and follow-up, one can do various things. Study and be critical of, but do not despise, the lavishly illustrated "coffee table" your richer friends can buy, or the African tourist art that other friends have brought back from the airports and big hotels in Africa. As general preparation, it is good to read such books as Robert Brain's *Art and Society in Africa* (London: Longmans, 1980), Robert F. Thompson's *African Art in Motion** (Berkeley and Los Angeles: University of California Press, 1974) and his *Black Gods and Kings** (same publisher, 1971), and some of the many other books on African art that have appeared in recent years. Details will be found in Eugene C. Burt's *An Annotated Bibliography of the Visual Arts of East Africa*[†] (Bloomington: Indiana University Press, 1980) and Dominique C. Western's *Bibliography of the Arts of Africa*[†] (Waltham, Mass.: African Studies Association, 1975). Above all, it is worth browsing through *African Arts*, the quarterly journal published by the African Studies Center of U.C.L.A.

The best lead into the music is J. H. Kwabena Nketia's *The Music of Africa** (New York: Norton, 1974), followed up by Elizabeth May's *Musics of Many Cultures* (Berkeley and Los Angeles: University of California Press, 1980).

Even if your teachers have told you that you cannot draw, keep a sketchbook and paint it in on your return home. If you are a camera buff you can make your own slides, or perhaps you can borrow slides and photos. Then produce a slide and music show for your friends or fellow students. The following groups, among others, produce slides and pictures that you may buy or borrow through your school: The Museum of African Art of the Smithsonian Institution, Washington, D.C.; the African Studies Program of the University of Wisconsin at Madison; and the Museum of Cultural History at U.C.L.A. University Prints of Winchester, Massachusetts, will make up books of selected prints from their excellently catalogued archive at the customer's request and at remarkably low prices.

Make your own collection of discs and music. It is singularly hard for someone with research training to know which discs to borrow or buy, because date and place of recording, let alone details of speed and method of first recording, are often lacking. Alan P. Merriam, *African Music on LP, an Annotated Discography* (Evanston, Ill.: Northwestern University Press, 1970), with its sixteen indices, remains the best guide to the early and vital recording period. It can be followed up with Elizabeth May's *Music of Many Cultures* (Los Angeles and Berkeley: University of California Press, 1980), J. H. Nketia, *The Music of Africa,* (New York: Norton, 1974), and the periodical *African Music*.

The following are a few random discs from the classical days of recording in Africa. They have been well tested in the classroom and are readily available.

Religion among the Yoruba

Folkways, Englewood Cliffs, New Jersey: FE 4441 *Drums of the Yoruba*, 12", 33⅓ r.p.m. Collected and edited by two pioneer names in this kind of work—William Bascom and Harold Courlander. Recorded at the courts of the king and chiefs of Oyo—the St. Peter's of the Yoruba gods. Festival music for *Òrìṣà*.

London Records, New York: LL533 *The Negro in Sacred Idiom*, 12", 33⅓ r.p.m. (dated to 1952). Fela Ṣọwande at the organ plays renderings of Yoruba sacred melodies, dirges, and dances, as well as traditional religious melodies used for basic ancient Christian worship, such as the Lord's Prayer and Kyrie. Remarkable Yoruba versions of "Go Down

Moses" and "Joshua the Son of Nun" bring those spirituals back to the homeland.

Columbia Records, New York: CL-1412 (CS 8210) Michael Babatunde Olatunji and band singing and drumming in a mixture of traditional and Western instruments. The pieces range from a chant to Ṣango the god of thunder to hymns of the United African Methodist Church. The whole has something of the spirit of the year of Nigerian independence. Recorded probably in 1960.

The Institute of African Studies, Ibadan, Nigeria, has released recordings of Yoruba operas that use traditional melodies and religious ideas. *Ọba kò so*, "The king did not hang," is about the alleged suicide of Ṣango. A transcription and translation by R. G. Armstrong was published by the University Press at Ibadan in 1968; a film of parts of the opera, in black and white, is available from the Indiana University A-V Center, Bloomington.

Religious Music of the Akan

Orpheum Productions, Inc., New York: Riverside RLP 4001—field recordings of African coast rhythms and tribal and folk music of West Africa. Recorded 1949. Includes talking drums, Anansi stories in Twi, traditional religious songs, as well as the use by Muslims in northern Gold Coast/Ghana of traditional religious melodies for Muslim purposes.

Decca, London: WAL 1001 *E.T. Mensah and His Tempo's Band*, 10", 33⅓ r.p.m. This band was at its best in the years leading to Gold Coast/Ghana independence in 1956. It plays jazz, high lifes, and calypsos, back home in Africa after travelling from St. Louis and Jamaica. Traditional religious melodies from the great Akan festivals are used for songs and for commemoration of St. Peter and the deeds of the witches of Kumasi.

Folkways, FW 8850 *Folk Music of Ghana*, 12", 33⅓ r.p.m. Recorded by Ivan Annan in Ghana in 1964; various local orchestras and choirs. The pieces range from Akan cult songs and dirges to the reuse of sacral king rhythms in honor of Kwame Nkrumah.

Hugh Tracey's regional *Anthology of African Music* is based on geography and the instruments used. In most of the ten records in the KMA Collection, sold by TMDP of Washington, D.C., there is something of interest. However, KMA 10 *Uganda* contains a fine collection of songs of sacral Ganda kingship by the kabaka's orchestra in its glory—before the kingship, which had survived colonialism, was swept away by an African government.

FILMOGRAPHY

The following annotated catalogs will be found useful: Steven Ohrn and Rebecca Riley, *Africa from Real to Reel, an African Filmography* (Waltham,

Mass.: African Studies Association, 1976); *Films on Africa,* 2nd ed. (Madison: University of Wisconsin African Studies Program: 1979); and Lori A. Baldwin, M. Kathleen Duttro, and Geza Teleki, eds., *Films, the Visualization of Anthropology* (Penn State University Audio-Visual Services: 1980). They give a full guide to the earlier masterpieces. *Encyclopedia Cinematographica* of Goettingen, Germany, distributed by Penn State, includes a series of short films about African traditional religion and ceremonies from all parts of the continent. Full notes and bibliographies in English are available.

A few masterpieces chosen at random:

African Religions and Ritual Dances, 19 minutes, color, 1971. A fine specimen, it features various Yoruba religious dances, including a fire dance associated with Şango.

The Great Tree Has Fallen, 22 minutes, color. The obsequies of Nana Prempeh II at Kumasi. A testimony to the survival of Akan tradition. Produced by the Canadian Broadcasting Corporation, 1971. Indiana University African Studies Program, University of Minnesota A-V Service, and others.

Fear Woman, 27 minutes, color. Woman's increasing role in religion and all walks of life in Africa as portrayed by United Nations experts. Chiefly focuses on Ghana. University of Michigan A-V Center, Ann Arbor, and others.

The Nuer, 75 minutes, color, 1971. The life and ceremonies of a section of the Nuer who live in Ethiopia. University of Wisconsin A-V Bureau, Madison, and others.

African Religions: Zulu Zion, 52 minutes, color, 1978. Number 10 of the B.B.C. Long Search series, this relates Zulu churches in South Africa to world religions.

African Sanctus, 47 minutes, color, 1977. Uses traditional music and shots of services in Africa to portray the Mass in Africa. Time-Life Films, New York.

Outside of our geographical limits, but a great masterpiece, are the *!Kung and /Gwi Bushman Film Studies.* These fifteen films were edited from the 500,000-plus feet of 16-mm film taken in the Kalahari during the 1950s. They are a monument to a way of life in which we all began and from which we still have much to learn.

PERIODICALS

The moving edge of the subject as a whole is in the periodicals and pamphlets. It is impossible to keep up with them. The following are generally available in university libraries and will give some clues as to what is going on: *Africa, African Arts, Journal of African History,* and *Journal of Religion in Africa.*

Glossary

Some say that any human thought can be expressed in the language of any human group, that the highest and most abstruse Iranian or Indic or Greek metaphysics can be put into Chinese, Urdu, Akan Twi, English, or the language of an indigenous group in northern Australia or Papua, New Guinea. However, there is an irreducible minimum of technical vocabulary in the great religions, and for scientific understanding we must refer to the original language of the idea, so far as we can find and understand it. For example, the same English four-letter word can serve as a euphemism for sexual intercourse and designate the overarching principle of God's attitude toward humanity and the universe in Christian thought—*love*. We do not know what word Jesus used, but the nearest we can get is *agape* in New Testament Greek. An exploration of its history and meaning is desirable for any student of Christian thought. The same could be said for certain basic words in Hinduism (for instance, *karma, dharma*), Judaism (*ts - d - q, q - d - sh, b - ṣ - r*, the roots from which we get the words usually translated "righteousness," "holiness," "body"), and so forth.

This glossary presents a few such words from Akan Twi, Yoruba, Dinka, Acholi, Kiswahili, and Luganda. ("Tribal" names, names of languages and places, anthropological terms, and words sufficiently explained in the text will be found in the general index.) For ease of reference we have alphabetized words according to the form of commonest use and not the root.

Abayifo (Akan Twi). The root is *bayi*, "bewitchment," hence the usual translation "witchcraft." Since *-fo* is the group affix and *a-* indicates a plural, the word refers to "bewitchment people," "witches," "wizards." It is hard in Akan usage to distinguish between "bewitchment" and "ensorcelling" (use of sorcery).

Abila (Acholi, Uganda). A shrine for the tabernacling of a spirit, often a little hut made of sticks.

Abosom (Akan Twi, Ghana; the singular is ɔbosom). "Spirits," "divinities." These include "children of 'Nyame" such as Bosomtwe, the sacred crater lake, and Tanɔ, the river (see index).

Abusua (Akan Twi). The family, the group that links itself back through the blood of the mothers to one foremother or ancestress (see *Mogya*). This blood yields not only relatives, from whom one expects and gives certain rights, duties, and privileges, but it provides part of one's soul-stuff.

Ajwaka (Acholi, Uganda). The healer, the psychiatrist; formerly translated "witch doctor." (See *Mganga*.)

Asamanfo (Akan Twi, Ghana; a plural of ɔsaman). The spirits of the virtuous and grateful dead. The affix *-fo* refers to a group of people, hence "spirit ancestors and ancestresses." Many great invocations begin *Nananom 'samanfo*, "O spirit grandfathers and grandmothers," and the drum beats take up the cadence. (See *Mizimu*.)

Asasewura (Akan Twi). The priest of the earth, the representative of the land. Often he was a person of autochthonous descent; that is, his residence in that place went back through his ancestresses to primordial time. A military or invading aristocracy might take over political and other power, but the disposal of the natural resources remained under the control of Mother Earth's mouthpiece.

Asuman (Akan Twi). Charms, amulets, "fetish" in its basic sense; storage batteries of power that are released on touch or at a prearranged moment.

Balubaale (Luganda). The *ba-* indicates a plural of persons; *lubaale* refers to certain major spirit-beings of the Ganda pantheon (see *Mukasa, Kibuuka* in the index). Clan spirits and many other types of spirits have generic names of their own. (See *Misambwa*.) It remains a puzzle whether Katonda, the creator spirit equated by local Muslims and Christians with God and Allah, is one of the *balubaale*.

Honhom (Akan Twi). "Oversoul," one of the six or eight types of soul or spirit that a human has. *Onyame honhom* is identified by Christian Ghanaians as the Spirit of God, but Twi is much more specific than either Greek or English when it comes to the science of spirit, pneumatology. (See also *Sunsum, Nkrabea, Ɔkra, Ntɔro, Abusua,* and *Mogya*.)

Jok (Acholi, Uganda). A generic term for a certain kind of spirit-power that can be localized in the shrines of the political unit (which the British called the "Chieftaincy"), in certain snakes or panthers, or in spirit-possession of humans.

Kungwi (Kiswahili). The senior woman who is called to teach a girl the meaning of menstruation and womanhood. She assists her through initiation, marriage, and divorce. The *kungwi* is confidante, tutor and mentor. She stands with the young woman in some sense against her parents and husband, yet she maintains the rules and norms of a society in which parents and husbands seem powerful.

Kwoth (Nuer, Sudan; the plural is *kuth*). An onomatopoeic word meaning "spirit." (We may compare the Hebrew *ruach*, the Greek *pneuma*, or the Latin *spiritus*.) Sir E. E. Evans-Pritchard said that the religion of the Nuer was not a polytheism but a "polyonomous (many-named) monotheism," because of the monistic uniting of all in *kwoth*. (Compare *atman* in Hinduism.)

Mchawi, Uchawi (Kiswahili). The root *-chawi* denotes "witchcraft." With the person affix *mu-*, the meaning is "practicer of 'witchcraft.'" (The *u* indicates the abstract noun, "witchcraft.")

Mganga (Kiswahili). The root is *-ganga*, which is in wide Bantu use. Basically the word indicates healing, setting aright, the restoration of balance. The colonial translation was "witch doctor," but "doctor" and "practitioner" are more appropriate. Sometimes the word *fundi*—"expert," "technician"—is used synonymously. (Compare *Ajwaka*.)

Misambwa (Luganda). Clan spirits and spirits connected with certain waterfalls and rocks. The root denoting this type of spirit is widespread in areas where Bantu languages are spoken.

Mizimu (Luganda). Spirits of human beings who have departed this life and are called to mind with reverence. They have many divine and superhuman powers, but are distinguished from divinities and clan spirits. The root is widely used in Bantu-speaking Africa in this specific way. (See *Asamanfo*.)

Mogya (Akan Twi). "Blood" (literally, it is plural, "bloods"). Used in talking of relationships, the word refers to the blood by which one is connected to one's mother, the mothers of one's line, the first foremother, the ancestress. Such blood is not something squalid of which one is ashamed, but is a source of strength and proper pride.

Mungu (Kiswahili). The Supreme Being. Used as equivalent to God and Allah. Cognate words are commonly used as names for the Supreme Being among a number of Bantu-speaking peoples, and this word is used along with several others. We may suppose that though the belief in a Supreme Being was universal and strong, in the earliest Bantu times it had not received definitive formulation. (See *Olódùmarè* and *Onyame*.)

Nkrabea (Akan Twi). Another constituent of the "psychology" or makeup of the spirit side of a human being. It refers to the characteristics we bring with us, our inborn personality. We do not owe this personality to heredity, and it is not the sum of the various parts of our spirits. (Compare *Fate*, Islamic *Qadar*.)

Ntɔro (Akan Twi). The "blood," in this case white blood, semen, which passes on the soul-stuff of the father and the ancestors.

Ɔkra (Akan Twi). The preexistent soul, the psyche, which is in every one of us.

Olódùmarè (Yoruba). A name for the Supreme Being that has a number of possible etymologies. Some Yoruba scholars suggest "The sole King who holds the sceptre of authority, is superlative in every respect, and is unchanging" as a beginning to which other attributes can be added. (Compare *Mungu* and *Onyame*.)

Onyame or 'Nyame (Akan Twi). The name of God, the Supreme, the Creator. The word is associated with the sky. Onyame is given the day-name Kwame (Saturday). The proverb says, *obi nkyere abrofra onyame*: "No one shows a child the sky/Onyame."

Òrìṣà (Yoruba, Nigeria). The major divinities of the Yoruba pantheon. They include Èṣù, Ṣàngó, Ògún, and others (see the index). (Compare the "children of 'Nyame" under *Abosam* and *Balubaale*.)

Pepo (Kiswahili). A type of spirit that becomes manifest in possession dances and reveals that it has created illness or caused the possessed to say or do certain things. The language does not give the word a prefix, so it is not in the person, thing, tree, or animal classes. With a locative (a termination indicating locality) it becomes *peponi*, "the place of the spirits." To Muslims this can be a word for Paradise. Presumably *pepo* is a very old African word for a kind of spirit, and indicates something very different from our popular notions, which are mainly anthropomorphic.

Sunsum (Akan Twi). A person's soul or spirit. This word is nearly equivalent to the word *personality*.

INDEX